WHAT LEADERS ARE SAYING ABOUT THIS BOOK

"This is a book I wish Bill Bright had written years ago, for if every church and every Christian individual were to put these proven methods to work on a daily basis, it could change the entire approach to world evangelization."

> **Billy Graham**
> **Billy Graham Evangelistic Association**

"I can think of no one better equipped and experienced—and burdened—to address this vital theme than my friend, Dr. Bill Bright. This is the most practical book on personal evangelism I have seen."

> **Ted Engstrom**
> **President, World Vision**

"So many are paralyzed by fear when it comes to confidently sharing their faith in Christ. Bill Bright cracks those barriers of fear with helpful advice and guidelines. WITNESSING WITHOUT FEAR is a valuable training tool for anyone who wants to effectively share Christ with others."

> **Joni Eareckson Tada**
> **Joni and Friends**

"The witnessing methods explained in this book are what a man used to introduce me to Christ in Washington, D.C. Since then, I have successfully applied these principles in my own witnessing opportunities. I can't speak highly enough of Bill Bright and the training he has provided the Christian world through this book."

> **Senator Bill Armstrong**
> **U.S. Senate, Washington, D.C.**

"Without realizing it, Christians often make their gospel presentations so cumbersome and boring that the message falls by the wayside. I heartily recommend WITNESSING WITHOUT FEAR as an effective back-to-the-basics approach that yields positive results."

Pat Robertson
Chairman, CBN

"In addition to a very credible approach to sharing Christ, WITNESSING WITHOUT FEAR contains one of the most practical chapters on praying for non-Christian friends and loved ones that I have ever seen. If you're praying for an unbelieving friend, neighbor or loved one, this book is for you."

Charles Stanley
Pastor, First Baptist Church
Atlanta, Georgia

"In his gentle yet compelling presentation of Christ's command to tell His good news, Bill Bright effectively puts in our grasp the tools to be Christ's witnesses."

Paul Crouch
President, TBN

"Is anyone as creative in leading people to Jesus as Bill Bright? His chapter on 'Conquering the Fear of Failure' is worth the price of the book. Every Christian fearful or nervous about witnessing *must* read this book!"

Ann Kiemel Anderson
Author and Speaker

"Every Christian knows that he should witness for Christ; most are paralyzed by fear. WITNESSING WITHOUT FEAR will prove a tremendous boon to all such Christians and will no doubt help to make vocal the silent majority."

D. James Kennedy
Coral Ridge Presbyterian Church
Ft. Lauderdale, Florida

Witnessing Without Fear

BILL BRIGHT

THOMAS NELSON PUBLISHERS
Nashville

Published in Nashville, Tennessee, by Thomas Nelson, Inc.

Scripture quotations marked TLB are from *The Living
Bible*, © 1971 by Tyndale House Publishers, Wheaton, IL
60187. All rights reserved.

Library of Congress Cataloging-in-Publication Data

Bright, Bill.
   Witnessing without fear / Bill Bright.
       p.   cm.
   Originally published: San Bernardino, CA : Here's Life
Publishers, 1987.
   ISBN 0-8407-4401-3 (pbk.)
   1. Witness bearing (Christianity) I. Title.
[BV4520.B65 1993
248.5—dc20   92-44081
                                      CIP

Printed in the United States of America

1 2 3 4 5 6 7 8 9 10 — 96 95 94 93

CONTENTS

FOREWORD

By Billy Graham

This is a book I wish Bill Bright had written years ago, for if every church and every Christian individual were to put these proven methods to work on a daily basis, it could change the entire approach to world evangelization.

Bill and I have been close friends for forty years. As brothers in the cause of Christ, we share the deep conviction that the world is more ready for the gospel of Jesus Christ today than ever before. More men and women than you ever imagined would say "yes" to the Savior if only someone would tell them how. And I believe that among that number may be some of your own family members, perhaps a neighbor or co-worker, or someone you don't even know yet—to whom God may lead you.

Yet, two obstacles prevent many Christians from telling others about Christ on a regular basis: fear and lack of know-how. In *Witnessing Without Fear*, Bill Bright effectively addresses both, and shows you how you can overcome fear to share your faith with confidence.

With a world so ready, the Christian community cannot afford to sit back and hope that the relatively few full-time ministers of the Word accomplish the task alone. The fulfillment of Christ's great command to "Go into all the world and preach the gospel to every creature" is the shared responsibility of every individual who calls Christ Savior and Lord.

Bill Bright has devoted himself to helping fulfill that great command. As president and founder of Campus Crusade for Christ International, he and his staff have introduced many thousands of students, laymen and women, government leaders, and others from all walks of life to our Lord. They have held Lay Institutes for Evangelism around the world to help train pastors and laypeople in effective witnessing techniques. Of the many fine evangelistic organizations about the Lord's work, few have been more effective in their outreach and discipleship training than Campus Crusade for Christ.

In the pages of this book, you will discover how God has used the obedient spirit of one shy, quiet servant of the faith to impact the lives of millions around the world. You will learn the same techniques for sharing Christ that have proven so effective over the years for Bill, his staff, and the people they have trained.

It is a privilege for me to recommend *Witnessing Without Fear* to every Christian who wants to find greater confidence and achieve greater results in telling others about Jesus Christ.

ACKNOWLEDGMENTS

The stories of Steve and Jackie, Al, Jill and Burt in chapter 1 are adapted from personal testimonies published in various issues of *Worldwide Challenge* magazine. "Burt" is not the doctor's real name.

Vonette Bright's story of receiving Christ with Dr. Henrietta Mears is reprinted from *Come Help Change the World,* Here's Life Publishers, 1985.

Senator Bill Armstrong's story of how he received Christ is adapted from his personal testimony published in *Worldwide Challenge* magazine, February, 1977.

All stories told in *Witnessing Without Fear* are true; in most cases, however, the names have been changed or withheld out of respect for the subjects privacy.

I am particularly grateful for Dan Benson's unselfish role in helping organize and write this book. His background as a former editor at *Worldwide Challenge* proved invaluable in communicating the heartbeat of the ministry of Campus Crusade for Christ.

Today's author faces a dilemma: The English language does not contain a one-word equivalent for "he or she." Yet it is cumbersome and impedes communication if an author repeatedly refers to another person as "he or she." Therefore, for the sake of readability, I generally will refer to another person as "he."

INTRODUCTION

Have you talked with anyone about Jesus Christ during the past week?

During the past month?

In the past year?

Since you became a Christian?

For almost forty years I have been involved in helping to train Christians across the country and around the world in how to share their faith in Christ more effectively. While I am encouraged at how large numbers of Christians are beginning to witness with confidence, our studies still show that the vast majority of believers—perhaps as many as 98 percent—are neither confident nor effective in their witness for our Savior.

There are several reasons why Christians don't witness, which we will address in this book. But the tragedy is that in failing to share one's faith, a Christian misses out on one of the greatest blessings our Lord offers: the profound joy of helping a fellow human being find new, abundant life, as well as eternal life, in Jesus Christ.

Most Christians, we've found, really *do* want to know how to give a clear, effective presentation of the gospel, but lack the practical know-how. If you are among them, I've prepared this book especially for you, to help you learn to share your faith with confidence.

The principles you are about to study have been learned in the crucible of front-line experience. In training conferences around the world, what you are about to read has changed multitudes of silent, guilt-ridden Christians into radiant witnesses for our Lord. Every story in this book is true, although in most cases I have changed or withheld the names of people involved out of respect for their privacy.

If you apply the proven concepts presented in the following pages, you, too, will become more effective in sharing Christ with your family, friends, neighbors, co-workers, and casual acquaintances.

I am praying for you—that as a result of your study of *Witnessing Without Fear*, you will receive new confidence and joy in telling others of our wonderful Lord and Savior, Jesus Christ . . . and that God will enable you to introduce many men and women to Him.

Bill Bright
President and Founder
Campus Crusade for Christ International

Christians just like you, from all
walks of life, are learning how to
share their faith in Christ effectively

❖ **1** ❖

YOU CAN WITNESS WITH CONFIDENCE

If I could show you how you can share your faith successfully, and with confidence . . . without alienating others or becoming someone you really don't want to be, would you be interested?

Witnessing for our Lord is something we all know we should do. From the pulpit on Sunday mornings we hear that we should "spread the Word in the marketplace." In our Christian magazines and books we read that our neighbors are hungry for the gospel—in fact, are dying without Christ. In God's Word we read the command of Jesus Himself to "Go into all the world, and preach the gospel to every creature . . ."

Yet, witnessing is an activity we frequently shrink from. To intrude in someone else's life seems not only threatening but blatantly presumptuous. We fear offending the other person, fear being rejected, fear doing an inadequate job of representing our Lord and even being branded a "fanatic."

So we remain silent, and pray that God will use someone else to get His message to those around us who do not know Him.

If you, too, have struggled with these fears, I have good news for you!

Christians just like you, from all walks of life, are learning how to share their faith in Christ effectively. Let me tell you about just a few of them.

"IT ALMOST SEEMED TOO SIMPLE"

Steve and Jackie became Christians after they were married. As they grew in their faith, they saw positive changes in several key areas of their lives, but one area that frustrated them was their inability to talk with people about their relationship with Jesus Christ.

"Then a friend suggested we attend a Lay Institute for Evangelism, designed for Christians who want to be more effective in sharing their faith," Steve relates. "Jackie and I thought, *What have we got to lose?*"

At the conference, Steve and Jackie learned how to witness for Christ using a very simple presentation of the gospel. "It almost seemed too simple," Steve says, "but since this method had proven effective for others, we decided to give it a try."

Soon, Jackie had led one of her neighbors to Christ, and was meeting regularly with her for follow-up Bible study and fellowship. A short while later, Steve had the privilege of leading his mother and Jackie's father to the Lord. Now they feel confident in witnessing to friends, business acquaintances and even people they've just met. They have introduced many others to Christ since they received those few hours of training in basic evangelism.

FROM SHY INTROVERT TO BOLD WITNESS

Al, a school custodian in Florida, says he has been an introvert most of his life. But "the Lord did a miracle" in his life a few years ago to give him the confidence he needed to tell others about Jesus.

"I would sit back and let somebody else do the work of reaching people for Christ," Al says. "But in 1980 my church sponsored a course in evangelism, which I attended. One of the men there, who had seen my faithfulness in helping with the church visitation program, asked me to come with him to a prison outreach.

"I went, and at the prison I met a guy and engaged him in a conversation. And I asked him if he'd like to receive Jesus as his Savior. He said 'yes,' and it floored me! I explained the gospel to him, and he became the first person who actually received Christ with me."

Now, Al shares his faith readily, as a natural part of his life. And people are responding. "One weekend the school where I work held a bazaar, and they had arranged for chicken dinners. At 8 A.M. on Friday a truck pulled up with six cases of chicken, and as I took the delivery guy to the refrigerator, I sensed the Lord telling me to ask him: 'Have you experienced the joy of knowing God personally?'

"He said 'no.' I explained the gospel to him, and fifteen minutes later, as we were standing together in the parking lot, he invited Christ into his life. The Lord had prepared him—it was just a matter of my bringing the subject up."

With just a small amount of training in how to witness without fear, Al had changed from a shy introvert to a bold witness for the Lord Jesus. And his sharing of his faith has been effective—hundreds of people in Jacksonville have been transformed as a result of Al's confident witness.

SHARING "THE MOST IMPORTANT THING IN MY LIFE"

Jill, a Minneapolis homemaker, wanted to somehow affect her neighborhood with God's love, but she became fearful every time she contemplated how to go about it. Then Joyce, a Christian friend with experience in personal evangelism, offered to give an evangelistic

Christmas coffee in Jill's home.

Jill agreed, but was so apprehensive she made Joyce promise not to make her do anything but serve the food. "I don't know how my neighbors will take this," Jill explained nervously.

When the coffee was over and the guests were preparing to leave, Jill spoke up. "May I just say something?" she asked, as tears of love came to her eyes. "I have lived in this neighborhood for five years, and I've dreamed of having you all in my home. And I've also dreamed of sharing the most important thing in my life with you, and that's my relationship with Jesus Christ. And, apart from this opportunity, I wouldn't have done it."

As tears streamed down Jill's face, the fifteen neighborhood women were crying, too. A real, ongoing ministry in the lives of those women began on that day as the Lord changed Jill from an uneasy observer to a bold communicator of God's love.

TRUSTING GOD WITH THE RESULTS

Burt, a general surgeon in Wisconsin, taught a weekly adult Sunday school class, counseled drug addicts, and had led several people to the Lord. He attended a Christian seminar for executives "rather self-complacent, fully expecting to counsel others rather than to be helped myself."

Part of the seminar dealt with how to reach others for Christ through a simple, straightforward presentation of the gospel. Burt determined that he would begin sharing Christ with each of his patients, "even if I just handed a booklet explaining the gospel to them with the remark that it had been meaningful in my life. I received some terrific responses."

Encouraged at his new-found effectiveness in witnessing, Burt decided to use these same methods in another arena. "I also work at the Addiction Center in my city, counseling heroin addicts. Before the seminar

I saw only haphazard results when I presented Christ as the only means of healing. I was trying hard in my own efforts and failing miserably.

"After the seminar I decided to present a simple gospel message and trust God with the results. When I asked a young man if he had ever investigated Christ's claims, he said he had been to church and rejected the whole thing. But when I asked him if *he* had actually done any investigating, he had to say 'no.' I shared the gospel with him, and he prayed with me, asking Christ into his life.

"At my suggestion he got a modern translation of the Bible. This aroused his mother's curiosity, and she came in to see me. When I told her that her son had become a Christian, tears came to her eyes, and she said that this was the answer to years of prayer."

Burt reports that, since the seminar, "I am seeing consistent results as others respond to God's love through my witness."

LED HER NEIGHBOR TO CHRIST

Kathy, a young commercial artist from Denver, was having a friendly visit with her next-door neighbor, Sue, when the subject of personal value systems came up. Kathy explained how, as a Christian, her value system was centered around Jesus Christ and the Bible.

"I've wondered about those things," Sue replied. "But they've never seemed very real to me. My only view of Christianity has been of 'religious fanatics,' but you don't seem to fit that mold."

Because Kathy had received some basic training in evangelism, she was able to give her neighbor a simple, non-threatening presentation of what Christianity was all about. Right there, in Kathy's back yard, Sue asked Christ into her life. She and her husband are now attending a thriving church in the area and are active in a couples' Bible study.

NOT A "BORN NATURAL" AT WITNESSING

Like many of these people, I have never found witnessing to come naturally and easily. Some of you may find this difficult to believe, but by nature I'm a shy, reserved person; initiating conversations with strangers is sometimes difficult for me. Even sharing the greatest news ever announced—that "God so loved the world that He gave His only begotten Son, that whoever believes in Him should not perish, but have everlasting life"—is not always as easy for me as you might imagine.

So it might seem incongruous that God called a shy young man thirty-five years ago to launch a small evangelistic ministry on the campus of UCLA, a ministry which would become Campus Crusade for Christ International. Witnessing, and training lay people and students and children to witness, is our primary calling. I don't even know if evangelism is my spiritual gift.

What I do know is that God has made it crystal clear in His Word that every Christian is to "Go and make disciples in all nations . . . and then teach these new disciples to obey all the commands I have given you . . ." (Matthew 28:19,20 TLB). I've tried to be obedient to this command, and God has honored my obedience. Like the people whose true stories I've shared in these pages, God has transformed my personal witness from one of shy hesitancy to one of confident initiative.

If He can do it for me, and for Steve and Jackie, Al, Jill, Burt, Kathy, and millions of others who have learned the important principles in this book, He can do it for you, too.

Never again will you need to be afraid that you'll be embarrassed in a witnessing situation.

Never again will you lack the essential Scriptures and key thoughts to share with an interested listener.

You'll find it more and more natural to begin a conversation about Jesus.

You'll know how to handle questions, distractions,

even objections.

You'll learn how to guide a person to a definite commitment to the Lord Jesus Christ.

And how to help the new believer begin to grow in his new walk with God.

If you're thinking at this point that "it may work for someone else, but not for me," you're not alone. We have seen thousands of Christians enter into this training totally convinced that it was not for them: It was too simple, they were too shy, or we "didn't know their situation." But they emerged from the training with their spirits rejoicing that God had transformed *their* witness, too, from shyness or complacency to confident initiative.

God will do the same for you.

Study the principles of this book with an open, eager mind.

As you read, continually pray that God would show you how to apply these principles in your own situation.

Practice the concepts you study with a Christian friend. (Or, if God so leads, with a non-believer. We've heard several testimonies of how Christians practiced these ideas with non-Christian friends, and the non-believers received Christ as their Savior and Lord on the spot.)

Begin to apply what you learn on a daily basis, just like the people in this chapter.

I'm confident you will be excited with the results. Soon, in spite of any failures or hesitancies of the past, you will be a more effective witness for our Lord.

Soon, you will be witnessing without fear.

❖ 2 ❖

THE STARTING POINT: LOVE & OBEDIENCE

"Why don't you come to church with us?" my landlords asked me, practically every time I saw
them.

For a long time, I would smile and thank this nice
elderly couple for the invitation and then come up with
an excuse. I had seldom attended church since I left
home for college, and I preferred to spend my Sundays
doing an amateur radio broadcast and going horseback
riding in the Hollywood Hills.

I had gone into business in Hollywood, California,
in the 1940s. And this godly couple, who must have
been in their eighties, were reaching out to me in probably the only way they knew.

They didn't know that their feeble efforts would
one day result in my receiving Christ. But let me dig-
ress a bit.

"FOR WOMEN AND CHILDREN ONLY"

My mother was a Christian, but my father was not a believer. So as I grew up in Coweta, Oklahoma, trying to take on the "macho image" of my father and grandfather, I thought Christianity was for women and children but not for men. I was determined that, in spite of my shy nature, I would be strong and self-reliant and accomplish anything I set out to accomplish.

When I went away to college, I was determined to become student body president, editor of the college yearbook, named to *Who's Who in American Colleges and Universities,* and graduate as the "Outstanding Student." In four years, I accomplished each objective. I was an agnostic, not knowing if God existed and not really caring whether He did. I believed that "a man can do anything he wants to, on his own." My father and grandfather had modeled that philosophy for me and I had proven it to myself in college.

But my ambitions didn't stop there. After college I was appointed to the faculty of Oklahoma State University. Since I had been reared on a ranch, I was assigned to serve as a member of the extension department, where I consulted with farmers and ranchers on various agricultural and cattle projects. I was paid many times what I was worth, but it wasn't enough. As a very materialistic young man seeking to prove myself, I wanted more.

TO LOS ANGELES

There were several career options open to me, but the most attractive was a move to Los Angeles where, through a series of events, I ended up in business for myself in Hollywood. That's where I met the charming, elderly couple who became my landlords.

"Why don't you come to church with us?" they continued to ask me. We lived right down the street from Hollywood Presbyterian Church, and this loving, white-haired couple seemed to take delight in attending the services.

"We have a great preacher by the name of Louie Evans," they persisted. "You'd love Dr. Evans."

Well, I couldn't imagine loving any preacher, but God was using this couple, in tandem with my mother's prayers, to sow a seed. One Sunday evening I returned from an afternoon of horseback riding, smelling like a horse myself, and I decided to drop in on the evening service. I arrived after the program started, sat by myself in the back row, and left before the service was over so no one would see me—or smell me.

So much for church. Or so I thought.

Apparently, my landlords had given my name to someone in the college department at the church. A few days later I received a call from a young woman with an appealing invitation:

"Bill, we're having a big party at (she gave the name of a famous movie star's) ranch and would love to have you join us. How about it?"

I couldn't think of an excuse quickly enough, so I ended up going. And I was in for quite a surprise. Gathered together in a big play barn were three hundred of the sharpest college-age men and women I have ever seen. They were happy, they were having fun, and they obviously loved the Lord. In one evening, my notion that Christianity is appropriate for women and children only was really shaken. I had never met people like this before.

Although very busy building my business (a fancy foods enterprise called "Bright's California Confections"), I began attending the college group's meetings at the church, along with regular church services. My shyness prevented me from mixing very much, and I always sat in the back. But I listened to what they were saying, and I fished out my long-unused Bible from a box of books and began to read and study on my own.

ONLY ONE WAY TO HAPPINESS?

There were a number of successful businessmen in the church, including a prominent builder who would invite small groups of young people to his home for picnics and a swim in his pool. During one of those popular events, we asked him about his business and what it was like to be so successful.

His answer startled me. "Material success is not where you find happiness," he stated firmly. "There are rich people all over this city who are the most miserable people you'll ever meet. Knowing and serving Jesus Christ is what's important. He is the only way to find happiness."

I recalled that this same principle had been exemplified by my godly mother. But somehow she hadn't verbalized it in a way that caught my attention, to make me realize my need to receive Him as my personal Savior and Lord. But she lived it—and now I was meeting sharp college kids and successful men and women who were living what my mother had lived, and had been taught how to verbalize their faith, too.

Over a period of months, I began to be greatly impressed with the eloquence and personality of Dr. Louie Evans. He presented Jesus Christ and the Christian life in an attractive way I had never known before. So, as a matter of intellectual integrity, I was forced to begin an in-depth study of the life of Jesus—and the more I read and studied, the more I became convinced that He was more than just a great historical figure. He was truly the Son of God.

"WHO ART THOU, LORD?"

One Sunday in 1945, Dr. Henrietta C. Mears, director of Christian education at the church, spoke to our college and young adult group about Paul's conversion experience on the road to Damascus. I had read the account before, but Dr. Mears made it come alive that evening as she told of this ambitious man who was committed to ridding the world of the new heresy called Christianity. She told how Paul (then Saul) had been thrown from his horse (something I could relate to) and blinded by a bright light. Saul then asked, "Who art Thou, Lord, and what wilt Thou have me to do?"

"And this is one of the most important questions you can possibly ask of God—even today," Dr. Mears told us. "The happiest people in the world are those who are in the center of God's will. The most miserable are those who are not doing God's will.

"Paul deceived himself into thinking he was doing God's will by persecuting the Christians. In reality, he was pursuing his own ambitions. So God set him straight through this dramatic experience on the road to Damascus."

As Dr. Mears spoke, I couldn't help noticing her wisdom, her boldness, and her love. She was another proof that my stereotype of Christianity had been all wrong. She spoke with authority, yet I could tell she held a genuine love for each of the young men and women in the audience.

"Now, not many of us have dramatic, emotional conversion experiences as Paul did," she continued. "But the circumstances don't really matter. What matters is your response to that same question: 'Who art Thou, Lord, and what wilt Thou have me to do?'"

She challenged each of us to go home, get on our knees, and ask God that all-important question.

COMPELLED BY LOVE

As I returned to my apartment that night, I realized that I was ready to give my life to God. I was not really aware of being lost, because I lived a relatively moral, ethical life. I didn't feel that I had an unfilled need. (I was indeed lost and in need, but was not aware of it at the time.) What attracted me most was God's love, which had been made known to me through my study of the Bible and through the lives of the people I had met at Hollywood Presbyterian Church.

I knelt beside my bed that night and asked the question with which Dr. Mears had challenged us: "Who art Thou, Lord, and what wilt Thou have me to do?" In a sense, that was my prayer for salvation. It wasn't very profound theologically, but the Lord knew my heart and He interpreted what was going on inside me. Through my study I now believed Jesus Christ was the Son of God, that He had died for my sin, and that, as Dr. Mears had shared with us, if I invited Him into my life as Savior and Lord, He would come in (Revelation 3:20).

Though nothing dramatic or emotional happened when I prayed, Jesus did come into my life. Asking Him that question, "Who art Thou, Lord, and what wilt Thou have me to do?", didn't seem very dynamic at first, but as I began to grow in my new commitment and love for the Lord, I became more and more aware of what a sinner I am and what a wonderful, forgiving Savior He is.

In time, I was elected president of the Sunday school class, and I met regularly with Dr. Mears and the other officers to pray together and discuss the profound truths of God's Word. And although I didn't realize it at the time, God was cultivating within me a desire to share with others the new life I had discovered in Christ.

MY FIRST WITNESSING EXPERIENCE

But God never has taken away my shyness. Maybe my reserved nature is my "thorn in the flesh," because as several friends have told me, people often expect the founder and president of a large international evangelistic ministry to be specially gifted by God to be outgoing, gregarious, and a natural conversationalist.

Perhaps God knew that if He made witnessing easy

for me, I might get the idea that it was my skill and not His working that brought people into His kingdom. This way, I have to be dependent on Him—and that's just the way He wants all of us to be, whether we're shy or not.

I sure had to depend on Him during my first witnessing experience, because I was scared to death. It was late 1945, and I remember it as though it happened just this morning (I guess when your adrenalin is pumping and your heart is in your throat, you remember things more clearly).

Bob was an outstanding young businessman who had just begun attending our church. As I became acquainted with him, I felt that the Lord wanted me to talk with Bob about his salvation . . . but I had no idea what I would say.

Maybe I can get Dr. Evans or Dr. Mears to talk to him, I rationalized. *They're good at this kind of thing. I'd probably blow it anyway.*

But I couldn't shake the uncomfortable feeling that for some reason, God wanted me—not Dr. Evans or Dr. Mears—to be the one. *But he's sharp*, I argued, *and he'll raise questions I can't answer. Or he'll say "no" and I'll be embarrassed.*

It's amazing, isn't it, how logical we can make ourselves sound when we're trying to justify our disobedience?

These sounded like good arguments at the time. But something kept reminding me of Matthew 4:19: "Follow me, and I will make you fishers of men." I realized it was my responsibility to simply follow the Lord and obey Him. His responsibility is to do the inner work of changing human hearts.

God also brought to mind Mark 16:15,16: "You are to go into all the world and preach the Good News to everyone, everywhere. Those who believe and are baptized will be saved. But those who refuse to believe will be condemned" (TLB). The more I rationalized, and the more I argued, the more God's Holy Spirit reminded me that this command of Jesus Christ is just that—a command. It is not optional. If we love Him, we obey Him.

So, with mouth dry and heart pounding, I spoke with Bob about inviting Jesus Christ into his life. As we sat in his car, half a block down the street from the front of the church, I told him my story, and showed him some Scriptures that highlighted man's need for God and how to receive Christ as one's personal Savior and Lord.

To my amazement and delight, Bob was as ready as anyone could be—as ripe as an overripe plum—and he prayed with me right there, asking the Lord Jesus to forgive him of his sin and to come into his life.

God had special plans for Bob. Shortly after he became a Christian, Bob resigned his position and entered seminary. He has been a minister for more than thirty-five years now, helping thousands of others trust Christ and grow in their walks with Him.

SHARING CHRIST WITH MY DAD

That first experience helped my faith grow to the point where I began to pray for my father. Dad had never gone to church. He loved and respected my mother, who went to church regularly and took the children with her, but he wouldn't have anything to do with the church.

I loved my father, and wanted him to realize what he was missing. So in the spring of 1946, I drove all the way back to Oklahoma to talk to him.

"Dad, I've discovered something that has really changed my life," I began, "and I'd like to tell you about it. Would that be all right?"

I could tell he was curious, although cautious. "Why, sure . . . I suppose so," he responded.

As we sat in the living room, I felt nervous. *What is he thinking, deep inside?* I wondered. *Will he resent his upstart son being so forward with him?*

I had been praying for him for months, and now I prayed a quick prayer for help. *Lord, there's no turning back now! Help me present You to my dad accurately, and with confidence. And help Dad to be open to Your leading.*

"You know, Dad, how I have always kind of felt that Mother's religion was all right for her?" I began. "How church was good for our basic moral values but nothing to get real personal about?"

Dad agreed, still cautious of what I might be leading to. "We both worked very hard to bring all of you up right," he said.

"And you did bring us up right," I smiled, "and I really appreciate your love and guidance."

We chatted a while about my growing-up years, and laughed at some of the awkward times. There was a warm, reflective smile on Dad's face as we spoke. Then we talked about my business in California and the friends I had made in the church there.

"Dad, I've discovered that it's possible to know God personally," I ventured. "I began to study what the Bible says about man's relationship with God. It says that 'God so loved the world that He gave His only begotten Son, that whoever believes in Him should not perish, but have eternal life.' But it also says, 'All have sinned, and come short of the glory of God.'"

"I'm familiar with those things." Dad squirmed just a bit in his overstuffed chair. "I've heard them before."

"So had I," I agreed. "But I had never related those verses to my life. As I studied them, and other parts of the Bible, I began to realize how much God loves me—and you. He sent His Son Jesus to die on the cross for our sin."

"I've always lived a good, clean life," Dad said. His eyes looked past me at the drapes, then over at the bookshelves, then at the floor—but not at me. "I've never cheated anyone in my life."

LOVE, DON'T PREACH

My father was bringing up what I have since learned to be a common smokescreen: "I'm good, moral . . . isn't that enough to get me to heaven?" I wanted to be very careful that I didn't in any way make him feel that I was ungrateful or unloving. In fact, I loved him so much that it was all I could do to keep from preaching the salvation message to him, camp-meeting style. But I knew that, as it is with most family members and close friends, loving gentleness was the approach to take with my father.

"Dad, I found out that it comes down to a personal decision—a commitment of faith in Jesus Christ."

I picked up my Bible from a nearby endtable and moved to the footstool beside him, turning to Ephesians 2:8,9.

"The Bible says, 'For by grace you have been saved through faith; and that not of yourselves, it is a gift of God; not as a result of works, that no one should boast.'

"Most people think just like you, Dad—that living a good life is all that's necessary to get us to heaven. But God's Word says we've all fallen short of His standard. It's only through His grace that we can be saved, if we accept Him."

"What do you mean by *accept Him?*"

I turned to Revelation 3:20. "Jesus Christ Himself said, 'Behold, I stand at the door and knock; if any one hears my voice and opens the door, I will come in to him . . .' So it's simply a matter of inviting Jesus Christ into your life. That's what I've done, Dad, and I can't describe to you the deep-down joy and peace I've experienced since then. I've really felt God's love. And He has that same kind of love for you."

Dad studied his shoes, then worked at an imaginary loose thread near the knee of his trousers. He seemed much more open to the gospel than I had thought he would be. My excitement grew.

I felt sure he was going to pray with me right there, just as Bob had done in the car back in Hollywood. I decided I had said enough, that the next words should be Dad's. So I waited, watching him, trying to stay calm, and praying silently as he thought.

After several moments, he opened his mouth to speak. I leaned forward expectantly.

"I need to know more, and I need to think about it," he sighed. "But I want to thank you, Son, for talking to me."

DISAPPOINTED, BUT ENCOURAGED

So my father did not receive Christ on that trip. I was disappointed, yet it encouraged me that he had been so open. I continued praying for him through that spring and summer, and since I had arranged to attend Princeton seminary that fall, I wrote home that I would be in Coweta for a three-day stopover enroute to Princeton, New Jersey.

My mother wrote back that during that same week, the tiny Methodist church in town would be holding a series of revival services.

Could this be the time my dad would give his life to Christ? I had a strong feeling—as if the Lord was assuring me—that this special revival campaign had to be God's special timing.

As I drove non-stop from California, I could feel the excitement building inside me. The service started at 7 P.M., and I arrived home at 6.

"Are you going to the church service?" I asked Mother and Dad, after I had greeted them.

"We hadn't planned on it," Dad replied.

"Would you go with Vonette and me?" (I had recently become engaged to Vonette Zachary, who had also been raised in the community.) Of course, Mother wanted to go. She looked at Dad.

"Sure, we'll go with you," he said.

The revival preacher was an old-fashioned

evangelist: He put lots of energy into his sermons, called sin sin and the devil the devil, and invited sinners to the front of the church during his altar calls. But he had been preaching for more than a week, with no response. Not one person had come forward to repent of their sins and receive Christ as Savior and Lord.

And this night was no different. "I feel God moving here tonight," he implored, "and if you aren't saved, God is telling you to come down here and turn your life over to Him. Now while we sing this next verse, come to the altar and give your life to Jesus Christ."

As we sang, I prayed for my father. I had left Mother and Dad at the church and rushed to pick up Vonette, and by the time we arrived, the church was full. We had found two seats on the side of the sanctuary opposite my parents. Now, as we sang the hymn, I watched out of the corner of my eye.

End of the first verse. No one had moved.

The preacher spoke again, perspiration glistening from his brow: "Do you have a loved one who is here and not a believer, and you've been praying for him? Get out of your seat and go put your arm around him and bring him to the altar."

I have never been one who likes to use pressure or coercion of any kind. And at first I cringed at what the preacher suggested. Within just a few moments, however, I sensed the Lord telling me to go talk with Dad.

But, Lord, I reasoned, *the Bright family is well known in this community, and Dad has a lot of pride. This is going to embarrass him. Do You really want me to do it?*

God must have known that I still had the tendency to let cowardice get the best of me, for before I could argue further I found myself out of my seat and walking all the way across the church toward Dad.

I put my arm around him. "Dad," I whispered, "come with me to the altar."

He did, and Mother joined us.

I didn't know then what I know now about leading a person to Christ. So Dad and I both knelt at the altar and wept while the preacher led the audience in another verse of the hymn. Dad cried and I cried, and I urged him to ask Jesus into his heart, but he didn't. Jesus was knocking at the door, but Dad didn't know how to open it.

No one else had responded to the invitation, so the service ended. I took Vonette to her home, then rushed home to talk to Dad.

He didn't talk much, and I knew better than to press him. But something from our brief words that evening stands out to me today, even though I didn't recognize it then.

WAITING TO "BREAK THROUGH"

Dad had been looking for an emotional experience. His stereotyped idea of a Christian conversion was one of lightning bolts from the sky or of being knocked off a horse like the apostle Paul. Since that type of thing hadn't happened at the altar, Dad didn't feel he had "broken through."

The next night, it happened all over again. A rousing sermon. An altar call. The preacher urging us to "put your arm around a loved one and bring him to the altar." My long walk across the church sanctuary. And my dad and me walking to the altar, with Mother alongside us, and kneeling and weeping at the front of that church.

As we knelt, Vonette joined us. And this time, my father invited Jesus Christ into his life wholeheartedly, unreservedly. I saw a visible change in his eyes, from complacency to joy. Then he thanked God for entering his life and beginning the change process.

But Dad wasn't done yet. He got off his knees and went back to where he had been sitting. He put his arm around a young man and invited him to join us at the altar.

That young man was my brother, who had just returned from the war in Europe. (He did not come forward that night, but years afterward he assured me that he had later received Jesus Christ as his personal Savior and Lord.)

ENJOYING ETERNITY WITH THE LORD

My father was a changed man after that night, and he lived thirty-six more years as a child of God before he went to heaven at age ninety-three. Eventually, my entire family came to Christ.

When I look back on how God brought me into His kingdom and began even then to show me how hungry people are to know Him, a key thought stands out to me: *All it took to begin my move toward God was the love and initiative of a few caring people.*

●My mother, who prayed for me every day.

●One elderly couple, who loved the Lord and their church. They probably didn't know how to witness, but they personified love to me and invited me to their church with them.

●An invitation to a barn party. And a group of caring, fun-loving Christian men and women who welcomed me with open arms.

●One dynamic, older woman by the name of Henrietta C. Mears, whose love for me and whose knowledge of the Scriptures made me want to know God's Word, too.

●Several Christian businessmen, who believed in hard, honest work for an honest profit, but exemplified the truth that real success comes only in knowing Jesus Christ.

●Dr. Louie Evans, the pastor of Hollywood Presbyterian Church, whose consistent lifestyle and intelligent teaching and preaching of the Scriptures attracted me to the person of Jesus Christ.

As I think of these people and their influence on me, I realize that God has indeed called each of us to personify Jesus Christ to the people with whom we come in contact every day.

Loving others, showing them Jesus Christ in word and deed, is not a job for pastors or ministry workers only. It's a joyful task to which God has commissioned everyone who calls himself a Christian.

To whom is God leading you today, to show love, to share the gospel?

Chances are, you'll be just as nervous as I was when you begin to share your faith. But my early experiences showed me that you don't have to wait until you feel "expert enough." It surely wasn't my expertise that led Bob and my father and eventually other members of my family to Christ—it was simply the fact that I wanted to obey God, who prompted me to share my faith with them. I was so awkward at first, but God worked His will in spite of me.

The keys were—and are—love and obedience. Despite my faltering nervousness, God spoke to these people. And you can have the same confidence that, if you reach out in genuine love, God will use you—no matter how nervous you may feel.

SUMMARY

●God has called each of us to personify Jesus Christ to the people with whom we come in contact every day.

●Personifying Christ involves loving others—in both word and deed.

●We are to follow Jesus, in obedience to His commandments. He expects us to obey His command to "Go into all the world, and preach the gospel to every creature." As we obey, we can trust Him to do the inner work of life-change in the heart of the person with whom we share the gospel.

●No matter how inadequate or nervous you may feel, God will use your witness to His glory when you take the initiative, in love, to share Him with others.

FOR REFLECTION AND ACTION

1. Make a list of people with whom you come in frequent contact: family members, friends, co-workers, neighbors.

2. Begin today to pray regularly for each person on your list, that the Holy Spirit would prepare their hearts to recognize the need for Jesus Christ.

3. During the next month, take the initiative to share a special act of love with each person on your list. A friendly phone call, a listening ear, a homemade batch of cookies, a helping hand, an invitation to lunch or dinner.

4. Is there someone on your list whom the Lord is leading you to invite to church or to a special Christian activity—as my landlord couple did for me several decades ago?

5. Pray and watch for that opening which will enable you to invite each person to receive Christ. You will learn how to do so as you continue to read.

*Five compelling reasons
why Christians should witness as a
way of life*

❧ 3 ❧

WHY WE CANNOT REMAIN SILENT

H ave you ever felt hesitant to share the gospel because you thought the other person simply would not be interested?

Have you ever sensed the Lord leading you to witness to someone, but you heard a small voice telling you, *You'll only start an argument?*

Or have you been slow to share your faith because you didn't feel you have the gift of evangelism, and witnessing is better left to those with "the gift"?

These are emotions which every Christian has felt at one time or another. I certainly have struggled with them. However, during more than forty years of sharing Christ and training others to do the same, I have been unable to find any biblical rationale to justify those reasons for not witnessing. In fact, from my personal experiences and studies of God's Word, five key concepts have been made clear to me—concepts which impact the lives of every Christian.

1. Christ has given a clear command to every Christian.

Jesus Christ's last command to the Christian community was, "You are to go into all the world and preach the Good News to everyone, everywhere" (Mark 16:15, TLB). This command, which the church calls the Great Commission, was not intended merely for the eleven remaining disciples, or just for the apostles or for those in present times who may have the gift of evangelism.

This command is the duty of every man and woman who confesses Christ as Lord. We cannot pick and choose which commands of our Lord we will follow. As Harold Lindsell wrote in *The Lindsell Study Bible*, "The evangelization of the whole world is the church's primary mission."

2. Men and women are lost without Jesus Christ.

Jesus said, "I am the way, and the truth, and the life; no one comes to the Father, but through me" (John 14:6). God's Word also reminds us, "There is salvation in no one else! Under heaven there is no other name for men to call upon to save them" (Acts 4:12, TLB).

When I spoke to several hundred students at an evangelistic event in Minnesota, several of them gathered afterward to ask questions. As I counseled them, I noticed an angry young student from India impatiently pacing back and forth.

When I finally was able to interact with him, he practically exploded at me. "I resent you Christians!" he spat out. "You are arrogant, narrow and bigoted. I am a Hindu—I believe that Christianity is one way to God, but you Christians are not willing to believe that *my* religion is one way to God."

"I am sorry if I have offended you," I apologized. "But I must remind you that 'I am the way, the truth and the life; no man cometh unto the Father, but by me' was a claim that Jesus Christ made for Himself. What do you think of Jesus?"

He thought for a moment. "I would have to say He is the greatest man who ever lived."

I learned from this young man that he was working toward a double doctorate in physics and chemistry. As we talked, I explained more about the claims Jesus made for Himself, how He died for our sin and was raised from the dead, and how His life demonstrated that He was indeed the Son of God. The young man's anger subsided.

"Now tell me," I said, "do you believe that 'the greatest man who ever lived' would lie about Himself? Or do you believe He was a deluded lunatic who just *thought* He was the only way to God?"

The young scholar realized the logic of John 14:6. His countenance changed, as if sunlight had broken through fierce storm clouds in his heart. "Would you like to receive Christ as your Savior and Lord?" I asked. "Yes, I would," he replied. "I understand it now." What a thrill it was to see this brilliant young scholar invite Jesus Christ into his life.

Men and women are truly lost without Jesus Christ. According to God's Word, He is the only way to bridge the gap between man and God. Without Him, people cannot know God, and have no hope of eternal life.

3. Rather than being "not interested," the people of the world are truly hungry for the gospel.
In the early 1960s, I was in charge of the student phase of the Bob Pierce Tokyo crusade. There were approximately 500,000 college students in the city, and I was scheduled along with several Campus Crusade leaders to speak at numerous meetings. I was told that nothing like this had ever taken place in Japan, so I boarded the plane with great excitement at the opportunity to present Jesus Christ to the Japanese student world.

FROM ENTHUSIASM TO DISCOURAGEMENT

Upon arrival, however, my enthusiasm turned to discouragement. We were briefed by a missionary who had been working in Japan for fifteen years.

"Now the Japanese are different," he warned. "They don't receive the Lord like Americans do."

He went on to explain that a Japanese would normally spend ten, fifteen, twenty years "seeking God" before receiving Christ. They would spend all this time in Bible classes, studying diligently, learning all the proper information about Christianity . . . making salvation a life-long quest rather than a decisive commitment.

I went back to my room after the briefing, downcast at the prospects of an unsuccessful evangelistic crusade. *Lord*, I prayed, *do You really want me here? I mean, I have so much to do back in the States, and if people here are not interested, maybe someone else could do what I'm doing . . .*

As I prayed, I sensed a peace coming over my troubled heart. Pascal's famous statement came to mind: "There is in the heart of each man a God-shaped vacuum, which cannot be filled by any created thing; but only by God the creator, made known through Jesus Christ." It was as if God were assuring me that the Japanese were like anyone else—hungry for God.

The next morning, I spoke in my first meeting to approximately one thousand students. For one hour, I presented the gospel and told stories to illustrate how people's lives have been changed by the power of the living Christ.

At the end of the hour, I said, "We're going to take a five-minute break. If you would like to receive Christ as your Savior and Lord, remain in your seat. The rest of you are free to go without any embarrassment. I'll then explain for another hour how you can be sure Christ is in your life and how you can grow spiritually."

The meeting was over. But nobody left.

So I spoke for another hour, walking the audience point-by-point through the gospel message. "Now," I concluded, "we've seen what the Bible tells us about why we need to accept Jesus Christ as our personal Savior and Lord. And you can invite Christ into your life this morning, through a simple prayer. If these words express the desire of your heart, pray with me silently, sincerely:

"Lord Jesus, I need you. Thank you for dying on the cross for my sins. I open the door of my life and receive You as my Savior and Lord. Thank You for forgiving my sins and giving me eternal life. Take control of the throne of my life. Make me the kind of person You want me to be."

I asked the students to raise their hands if they had prayed that prayer. Almost every hand went up.

THE END OF A LIFE-LONG SEARCH

I practically ran back to my hotel to see the missionary who had briefed us. "Most of those students accepted the Lord!" I exclaimed.

"Aw, Bill, you're an American. They don't want to offend you," my missionary friend said, as gently as one can possibly be when throwing cold water on you. "You see, these people appreciate General MacArthur's benevolent treatment of the Japanese after the war. And since you're an American, they don't want to offend you, so they'll do anything you ask them to do."

Again, my balloon deflated. So the next day I went through a similar procedure, with a new group of students. I spoke for an hour, then gave a clear invitation for those who wanted to receive Christ. "Now ladies and gentlemen," I concluded, "I'm told that you're staying in these meetings just because you want to be gracious to me—you don't want to offend me because I am an American. But if you've received Jesus Christ into your life today and you know without a doubt that He is in your life, I want you to come and tell me.

"Don't do this if you're just wanting to be courteous to me. Take my hand and tell me the truth, in your own words. I want to know for sure."

And the line formed. I shook hundreds of hands that morning, but more importantly I had the thrill of looking into the glowing faces of young men and women who had just ended their life-long search for spiritual truth.

People are indeed hungry for the gospel. Jesus said, "Do you think the work of harvesting will not begin until the summer ends four months from now? Look around you! Vast fields of human souls are ripening all around us, and are ready now for reaping" (John 4:35, TLB).

IN "THE HOUSE OF BEAUTIFUL WOMEN"

Shortly after Vonette and I began working with college students at UCLA, we were scheduled to speak at the Kappa Alpha Theta sorority on campus. At that time, the student newspaper and student government were controlled by the radical left due to active communist recruitment activity on campus. As I prepared to speak, I prayed hard that God would break through this atmosphere and reach at least one or two of the young women.

The sorority was called "the house of beautiful women," and they were. Sixty of them gathered in the living room to hear us speak, and when I finished my message I said, "If you would like to know Jesus Christ personally, come and tell me."

I had prayed for one or two. But at least thirty of these beautiful college women stood in line to tell me they wanted to become Christians.

Since this was my first group meeting in which people wanted to receive Christ, I didn't know what to do. So I did what any good businessman does when he's not sure what to do: I called another meeting.

"Vonette and I would like to invite all of you to

our home tomorrow night," I announced. "We'll talk more about how you can know Christ personally. Would you come?"

Each of the women agreed, and most of them came—some with boyfriends. All but a few prayed with us that evening, yielding their lives to Christ. From this nucleus the ministry called Campus Crusade for Christ was born, and spread not only across the UCLA campus but across the country and around the world.*

These sharp young women and their boyfriends were hungry for the good news. They were waiting only for someone to tell them, someone to show them how.

IN WASHINGTON, D.C.

A few years ago I was concluding a meeting with a group of executives when one came up to me. "Bill," he said, "next time you're in Washington, would you please go see my senator? He needs the Lord."

The question startled me. "Don't you think that would be presumptuous, going to see a senator, without an appointment, to talk to him about the Lord?"

"Tell him I sent you," my executive friend laughed, for he knew that his senator probably didn't even know him.

Several months later, I was in the Senate office building in Washington where I met and prayed with a couple of other senators. As I walked down the hall, I saw the name of the senator to whom I had been referred.

By this time, I had learned not to argue with the Lord. The natural man in me would have said, *Who do you think you are, bothering the senator—and he probably won't even be interested!* But over the years, God

_____

*For the complete Campus Crusade for Christ story, see *Come Help Change the World* (Here's Life Publishers, 1985).

had taught me to be prepared for Him to provide un-
usual witnessing opportunities, sometimes in the most
unlikely circumstances. And, He doesn't expect eloquence, just obedience.

So, with a quick prayer for God's guidance, I entered the senator's office.

"May I help you?" the receptionist asked.

"Good morning. My name is Bill Bright, and I'd
like to talk to the senator," I said.

"Let me see," she said as she left her desk and
disappeared through a doorway to the back offices.

In less than a minute, she was back. "He'd be glad
to see you right now," she reported.

In most circumstances it's best to take the time to
converse and establish a good rapport with the person
you're sharing Christ with. However, since I had arrived without an appointment, I wanted to respect the
senator's time constraints. I got right to the point.

"It's an honor to meet you, Senator," I greeted, as
we shook hands. "I'm Bill Bright."

"Bill, it's good to meet you," the senator smiled.
"Have a seat there. How is your stay in Washington?"

"I'm having a good visit. I'm president of Campus
Crusade for Christ International, and I've been here to
meet with several government leaders who have committed themselves to Jesus Christ. Senator, are you a
Christian?"

That question, *Are you a Christian?* could come
across as blunt and insensitive. Yet, I have found that
if I bathe an opportunity in prayer, and if I make sure
God is on the throne of my life and I'm reaching out
in genuine love in the power of the Holy Spirit, the
person I'm sharing with invariably responds to this
question without taking offense. Such was the case with
this busy senator.

"I don't know—I think so," he hesitated. His voice
was quiet, and he leaned forward, eager to hear more.
His contemplative, brown eyes looked straight into
mine.

"If you were to die tonight, do you know without a doubt that you would go to heaven?" I asked.

His gaze dropped from me to the top of his desk. "No," he whispered. "I don't."

"You'd like to know, wouldn't you?" I asked.

"You bet I would."

I went through a brief presentation of the gospel, and the senator responded that he would like to receive Christ.

DON'T BE SELFISH WITH THE GOOD NEWS

Indeed, vast fields of human souls are ripening all around us, and are ready now for reaping. We must assume that the family member, neighbor, co-worker, or person we've just met will be interested in the good news we have to tell. He may have just gone through a set of circumstances that has prepared his heart to receive Jesus Christ. God may have been leading him into an awareness of his need for truth. Perhaps he has felt especially alone or in need of love.

Can we afford to be selfish with the gospel, when there is overwhelming evidence that the majority of people are hungry for God? As Jesus said, "The fields are ripe unto harvest."

4. We Christians have in our possession the greatest gift available to mankind—the greatest news ever announced.

Christ is risen! We serve a living Savior, who not only lives within us in all His resurrection power but has assured us of eternal life. He died on the cross in our place for our sin, then rose from the dead. We have direct fellowship with God through Jesus Christ. And this fellowship, this peace, this gift of eternal life, is available to all who receive Him.

Why are we so hesitant to share this good news? Why is it that we so readily discuss our political views or athletic preferences, our gas mileage or utility bills, our children's growing pains or our office gossip, but clam up when it comes to discussing the greatest news ever announced?

OUR NUMBER-ONE MESSAGE

If our faith in Christ really means as much to us as it should, then it only follows that our faith should be the number-one message on our lips. People *want* to hear good news. And when you present it properly and with love, you will usually see a positive response.

Several years ago, a group of young Christians were singing Christmas carols in Hollywood and Beverly Hills. They had called to make appointments to sing in several TV and movie stars' homes, and then after singing they left behind a letter I had written about Jesus and how one can know Him personally.

One actor—well-known for his lead roles in two long-lasting family TV series—was particularly gracious to the carollers, and the next day he called the group leader.

"I've read this letter a dozen times," his voice boomed over the phone. "I've never read anything so wonderful. Could I meet Mr. Bright?"

The group leader gave my office the message, and I called the gentleman.

"Mr. Bright—"

"Please, call me Bill," I interrupted. "I've watched your shows enough to feel like I know you already."

"Bill, I know you must be very busy," he apologized. I could sense a feeling of awkward determination in his voice. "I really must see you. I don't want to impose on you, but would you please take a few minutes and see me?"

We arranged for him to meet me at my home. After unfolding himself from his expensive antique car, he bounded up the steps to greet me with a firm handshake and his familiar smile.

"I've been reading your letter and it's been very meaningful to me," he began, after we had chatted for a few minutes over iced tea. "I've been a member of the vestry of my church for years, but I've never read anything like your letter. I don't know Christ personally, and I want you to help me."

We talked briefly about the content of the letter, but he didn't need convincing. He was ready. We got on our knees at the sofa in the living room, and he prayed the most beautiful, heart-warming prayer for salvation I have ever heard. Then, as we stood, he gave me a bear hug that almost cracked my ribs. He went away as delighted as a child at Christmas.

The Scriptures make the good news so clear:

●"But to all who received him, he gave the right to become children of God" (John 1:12, TLB)

●"For God so loved the world, that he gave his only begotten Son, that whoever believes in him should not perish, but have eternal life" (John 3:16).

●"For he has rescued us out of the darkness and gloom of Satan's kingdom and brought us into the kingdom of his dear Son, who bought our freedom with his blood and forgave us all our sins" (Colossians 1:13,14, TLB).

5. The love of Jesus Christ for us, and our love for Him, compels us to share Him with others.

Jesus said, "The one who obeys me is the one who loves me" (John 14:21, TLB). In other words, He measures our love for Him by the extent and genuineness of our obedience to Him. And as we obey, He promises He will reveal Himself to us: ". . . and he who loves Me shall be loved by My Father, and I will love him, and will disclose Myself to him" (John 14:21).

What are we to obey? When it comes to witnessing, we have the specific commandment from Jesus Christ: "You are to go into all the world and preach the Good News to everyone, everywhere." Helping to fulfill Christ's Great Commission is both a duty and a privilege. We share because we love Christ. We share because He loves us. We share because we want to honor and obey Him. We share because He gives us a special love for others.

IS ANYTHING MORE IMPORTANT?

As a corollary to that specific commandment, we are also called to be obedient to God's daily guidance as He brings us in contact with people from all walks of life. We've all experienced that special feeling—that whisper deep inside telling us: *Tell this person about Jesus Christ.* But, for one reason or another (fear, rushed schedule, not knowing what to say) we're tempted to neglect the whisper and proceed with "more important things."

I was in such a hurry to do something "more important" one fall day that I almost missed out on a real blessing that God had waiting for me. I was driving to speak to a group of Christian college students at Forest Home, a beautiful conference center in the San Bernardino mountains. The uphill climb proved a little strenuous for my car, however, and the radiator started to boil over. I pulled into the driveway of a nice, rustic-looking house, which turned out to be the home of a man who worked with the forestry service.

"Can I be of help?" he smiled as he came over to my car. With a garden hose he filled the radiator, and we chatted while I let the engine run. Nervously, I stole several glances at my watch.

While we chatted, my radiator cap had fallen to the ground, and as I stooped to pick it up, my New Testament fell from my pocket. Hurriedly, I put the Testament back in my pocket, replaced the radiator cap, slammed the hood down, and hopped in the car.

"Thank you for the water!" I called out as I sped out of the driveway. *I might still make it on time*, I thought.

But almost immediately, a disquieting feeling overcame me. The Lord was telling me, *I wanted you to talk to him about Me.*

But I was cutting it awfully close getting to my speaking engagement. *It's too late*, I argued. *I can't go back now.*

I want you to go back.

But he'll think I'm crazy! What would I talk about?

I want you to talk to him about his soul. Go back.

But I'm already late for the meeting . . .

Go back.

So, after arguing with God for two or three miles, I turned the car around and went back. Down the mountain. Into the driveway.

"What can I do for you?" he asked. "Did you forget something?"

I got out of the car, closed the door, and leaned against the body of the car. "Yes sir," I answered. "I forgot to talk to you about Jesus."

His eyes looked straight into mine for a moment. "Come inside." He spun around to lead me into his house.

He had been active in church all his life, until several years before when an argument with a church member had prompted him to leave the church. Since then, he had had nothing to do with God.

"You know, it's a very interesting coincidence. There's a revival campaign going on in my old church. My wife has been going every night, but I haven't gone.

"But," he continued, "I've been thinking about what I've been missing. And I believe God sent you back just to give me the added encouragement I need to get my life straightened out with Him."

He called his wife in from the kitchen to join us. "Would you pray with us—for me?" he invited. We got on our knees, and I remember the man's wife shedding tears of joy as her husband asked the Lord to forgive him for his waywardness and to take control of his life from that moment on.

The Lord had prepared him. And on that particular day, it was more important to Him that I be a few minutes late for a meeting and touch a soul who was ready to renew his walk with the Lord.

THE "DIVINE APPOINTMENT"

We have a ringing command from our Lord to share the gospel, and men and women are lost without Him. Indeed, they are hungry for the good news, and we Christians have in our possession the greatest news ever announced. Our love for the Lord—and His love for us—compels us to obey Him as He leads us into the sharing opportunities of each day.

As you walk in prayerful fellowship with the Lord, always, whenever you're alone with someone, consider it a divine appointment. Always be ready to share your faith. It could well be that God has led that person to you, because you know the good news and that person needs to hear it.

SUMMARY

●People all around you are indeed hungry for the good news that Christ died for their sin. Without Jesus, they have no hope of knowing God or having eternal life.

●God opens up unique witnessing opportunities to you, and sometimes in the most unlikely of circumstances. He doesn't expect eloquence, but He does expect obedience.

●You have in your possession the greatest news ever announced. Why be so hesitant to share it with others?

●Christ has commanded us, "You are to go into all the world, the preach the Good News to everyone, everywhere." If we love Him, we will obey Him: "The one who obeys me is the one who loves me."

●Whenever you're alone with someone for a few minutes or more, consider it a divine appointment.

FOR REFLECTION AND ACTION

1. Like the well-meaning missionary in Japan, have there been Christians whose negative thoughts and comments have impeded your witness? Have you had a tendency to think negatively about how people might respond to you?

2. Take several moments to reflect on what your relationship with Jesus Christ means to you. Complete the statement, "Because Christ rose from the dead and lives in me, I . . ." Isn't this truly the greatest, most joyful news you could ever share with another person?

3. Based on your obedience to Christ's command to share your faith with others, what conclusion do you think He would draw about your love for Him?

4. Can you think of at least two people with whom God was leading you to share Christ during the past week? How did you respond?

There are three barriers
that can keep you from telling others
about Jesus Christ

✢ 4 ✢

WHY MORE CHRISTIANS DON'T WITNESS

"**I** don't wear my religion on my sleeve. My religion is personal and private, and I don't want to talk about it."

He was one of America's great statesmen—a Christian—and I had just shared with him a plan for world evangelism. As we talked about involving a thousand key Christian leaders in the effort, his statement startled me.

"You're a Christian, aren't you?" I asked him.

"Yes, I am," he replied. "But I'm not a religious fanatic."

I've heard this logic several times, and it grieves me every time I hear it. It grieved me that day as I heard this fine gentleman rationalize his passive faith.

I prodded gently: "Did it ever occur to you that it cost Jesus Christ His life so that you could say you're a Christian?"

He thought a moment, but didn't respond.

"And it cost the disciples their lives," I continued. "Millions of Christians throughout the centuries have

53

suffered and many have died as martyrs to get the message of God's love and forgiveness to you. Now do you really believe that your faith in Christ is personal and private and that you shouldn't talk about it?"

"No, sir," the man sighed. "I'm wrong. Tell me what I can do about it."

Without even realizing it, this Christian leader had fallen for one of Satan's favorite lines: that one's faith should be a very private thing, something you just don't talk about. As a result, his witness for Christ was next to nil. He had held in his possession the greatest news ever announced, but up to that point he had refused to share it.

As a ministry which specializes in helping train laypeople in effective evangelism, we have made extensive studies of why Christians don't share their faith more readily. We've found that, while some believe with my friend that "religion should be personal and private," most Christians do recognize the biblical imperative for a personal witness. But they allow three barriers to keep them from witnessing without fear.

BARRIER 1: SPIRITUAL LETHARGY

If you aren't excited about something, chances are you won't tell many people about it. And we find that in the lives of far too many Christians, the excitement of the Christian walk has been dulled by everyday distractions, materialistic pursuits and unconfessed sin. Like the believers in the church of Ephesus, these men and women have "left their first love."

A few years ago, following one of my lectures on the lordship of Christ, a bright young educator came to see me. His credentials were superb: an earned doctorate, an already-successful career, and prospects for even further upward mobility. But something was bothering him.

"I became a Christian several years ago when I was a young boy," he began. "But through the years I gradually took back the control of my life. I am still active in the church. Yet, I'm ashamed to say that I've been more interested in promoting my own business and social position than I have been in serving the Lord and getting to know Him better. I have compromised my business and professional standards, and have not always been honest and ethical in my dealings with others.

"God has shown me . . . that I have wasted many years living selfishly and for my own interests. Now I want to help reach the world for Christ."

We prayed together, and rejoiced in his new commitment. Up to that moment he had been living in spiritual lethargy: self-centered, carnal, and with little desire to reach out and share the love of Christ with others. Upon his re-dedication, however, he became a confident, effective witness.

If you have felt spiritually dry or defeated, it is possible that you have "left your first love" (*i.e.,* your total devotion and obedience to Jesus Christ). Perhaps you've allowed the hectic pace of life to distract you from quality times of prayer and meditation on God's Word. Perhaps you have allowed society's pervasive message of humanism and self-gratification to lure you toward "the good life" . . . and away from the best life. Perhaps these and other offenses toward God have festered into unconfessed sin.

In Psalm 66:18 we read, "If I regard iniquity in my heart, the Lord will not hear me" (KJV). Unconfessed sin short-circuits our fellowship with God and makes us like those Christians Paul describes in 1 Corinthians 3:1-3:

> And I, brethren, could not speak to you as to spiritual men, but as to men of flesh, as to babes in Christ . . . for you are still fleshly [carnal]. For since there is jealousy and strife among you, are you not fleshly, and are you not walking as mere men?

The carnal Christian described by Paul does not

feel constrained to share Christ because his attention is focused on himself rather than on others. He has allowed love of things, love of distractions, and unconfessed sin to take his eyes off Christ. He has left his first love.

If these symptoms describe your spiritual life, you can restore your first love—your intimacy and joy in the Savior—by taking two important steps.

1. Be sure there is no unconfessed sin in your life.
Wait quietly before God. Ask Him to reveal to you, through His Holy Spirit, any areas that are not right.

●Have you offended a friend, and not asked his forgiveness?

●Have you violated a command of God's Word, and not asked God's forgiveness?

●Have you lived in anxiety or worry? Cynicism or negativity?

●Have you been unloving to others at home, work, church or elsewhere?

●Have you been dishonest in your finances or work habits?

●Have you dwelled on lustful thoughts?

●Have you failed to tell someone about Christ when the Lord was prompting you to do so?

●Have temporal pursuits (work, money, pleasure, "things") dominated your thinking and lifestyle?

As the Holy Spirit brings these to mind, agree with God in prayer that you have sinned, and appropriate His forgiveness, promised in 1 John 1:9: "If we confess our sins, He is faithful and righteous to forgive us our sins, and to cleanse us from all unrighteousness."

To help you better understand the importance of confession, the original meaning of the word *confess* means "to agree with." As you agree with God concerning sin in your life, you are saying at least three things to Him: (1) "God, I agree with You that these things I'm doing (list them) are wrong"; (2) "I agree with You that Christ died on the cross for these sins"; and (3) "I repent—I consciously turn my mind and heart from my sins and as a result I turn my actions toward obedience to You."

2. *Be sure you are controlled by God's Holy Spirit.*

Walking in the Spirit is the secret of living the Christian life. It simply means allowing God, through His Holy Spirit, to empower and guide you moment by moment, day by day.

The same Holy Spirit who empowered the disciples at Pentecost to "turn the world upside down" is available to each of us, today. We are commanded in Ephesians 5:18 to be filled (controlled, directed, guided) with the Spirit. On the authority of God's promise that He will answer us if we pray according to His will (1 John 5:14,15), and since it is His will that we be filled with His Spirit, you can ask God right now, in faith, and He will fill you with the Holy Spirit.

Keeping Christ "On the Throne." To understand what is happening in your life, picture a large throne. This represents your "control center," or your will. When you received Christ as Savior and Lord, you invited Him into your life and onto the throne—you deliberately surrendered the control and guidance of your life to Him.

However, whenever you yield to temptation and sin, you take back control of that throne. Christ is still in your life, but He is no longer on the throne. God created you with free will, and He wants you to choose freely whether you obey Him.

The apostle Paul identified this problem when he wrote:

> "I don't understand myself at all, for I really want to do what is right, but I can't . . . But I can't help myself, because I'm no longer doing it. It is sin inside me that is stronger than I am that makes me do these evil things.
>
> "I know I am rotten through and through as far as my old sinful nature is concerned. No matter which

way I turn I can't make myself do right. I want to but
I can't" (Romans 7:15-18, TLB).

"Spiritual Breathing." Being filled with the Holy
Spirit is simply the act of again surrendering to God
the control of the throne of your life, by confessing sin
and accepting His loving forgiveness. This concept,
which I call "Spiritual Breathing," is one of the most
vital truths of God's Word. It is the key to daily victory
over the constant pull of sin in your life.

Just as we exhale and inhale physically, so we can
exhale and inhale spiritually. We "exhale" when we
confess our sins, and we "inhale" when we appropriate
the cleansing, control and power of God's Holy Spirit.

As a result of our training conferences, thousands
of people have told us that this one simple truth has
completely changed their walk with the Lord. Jeff, for
example, had been a Christian since childhood, but he
had felt frustrated with his "roller coaster" commitment to Christ. When he learned how to be filled with
the Spirit and keep God on the throne of his life through
Spiritual Breathing, he consciously began telling the
Lord, "I give you control of the throne of my life. Guide
me, and give me wisdom and strength today to act, talk
and think the way You want me to." From a life of
constant defeat, be began to live in the victory and joy
of our risen Lord.

It is the Holy Spirit who will convict you when
you've sinned; who will nudge you to extend a caring
hand to a neighbor; who will give you a reservoir of
love to give to others; who will urge you to share your
faith with the people around you. Your obedience to
His daily prompting will keep you from ever wanting
to leave your first love.*

---

*For a more complete discussion of the ministry of the Holy
Spirit in your life, see appendices B and C.

BARRIER 2: BELIEVING THE
ENEMY'S "LINES"

"We wrestle not against flesh and blood, but against principalities, against powers, against the rulers of the darkness of this world," Ephesians 6 tells us.

There is a definite spiritual battle raging. The Bible says that "God has liberated us out of the darkness and gloom of Satan's kingdom." Every Christian was once a member of that kingdom, and those non-believers with whom we share Christ are still members of Satan's kingdom. It's not a pleasant thought, but non-believers are there either by choice, ignorance or default and Satan is doing everything he can to retain his control.

So as you sense God leading you to tell someone about Jesus, Satan's agents go to work. You may even hear some very believable "lines" from his direction that are intended to make you think twice, turn heel, and abandon your good intentions.

"Mind your own business—you don't have any right to force your views on someone else."

When you hear this line, ask yourself: "Where would I be today if the person who introduced me to Christ had 'minded his own business'?"

When we share Christ in a gentle spirit of love, we aren't "forcing" our views on anyone. We speak gently and lovingly; the hearer is free to listen, change the subject, or move away.

How could I have possibly "forced" my views on the huge, 6'6" Marine seated next to me on the bus some time ago? I'm comparably small in stature, but I serve a big God who was leading me to share the gospel with this hulking, mean-browed man who literally towered over me as we sat side by side on that bus.

He told me he had just been released from the "brig" for slugging his commanding officer. But the more we talked, the more I felt he was hungry for God.

When I mentioned how God loved him so much that He sent His Son to die for him, he began to sob.

"My mother is a Christian and my wife is a Christian," he wept. "They've been trying to get me to become a Christian for years."

Then this big, tough-as-nails Marine said something I'll never forget: "I don't remember the last night I didn't wet the pillow with my tears because I'm afraid I'll die without God."

His mother and wife had told him he ought to become a Christian. But they had failed to tell him *how*. When I showed him how he could invite Christ into his life, he jumped at the opportunity. He was so thrilled that he left the bus at the next stop to call his mother and wife to tell them the news.

"You're going to offend this person. Don't say anything."

If someone you know were dying of cancer and you knew the cure for cancer, would you avoid telling him about the cure because you might offend him?

Of course not. You would gladly share the good news that his cancer can be cured. Why should we be any less enthusiastic about sharing the Ultimate Cure over the Ultimate Disease?

"He'll think you're a fanatic."

Yes, he might. But then again, he might be the one person whom God has specially prepared for you on this day. Not everyone will accept the gospel—even Jesus encountered men and women who rejected His message. Our role is not to convert, but to obey. We can disarm the "fanatic" stereotype with a confident, loving, logical presentation of the claims of Christ, shared in the power of the Holy Spirit.

"Distractions, interruptions. Interruptions, distractions."

The phone rings. Someone else enters the room. A

baby cries for attention. Someone turns on the TV set. When you set out to raid Satan's kingdom, you have to believe he will counterattack. He can engineer circumstances to place all kinds of obstacles between you and the person with whom you're sharing.

Whenever I find myself in such a situation, I pray silently, even as we're talking, that God would bind Satan and allow my friend to hear the message and make a free choice. It's definitely a spiritual battle, but you can be assured that if Satan is causing problems, he's worried. You must be doing something right.

"This person will say 'no,' and I'll be embarrassed."

We Christians are often guilty of presenting the gospel with an attitude that says, "Uh . . . you wouldn't want to receive the greatest Gift available to mankind, would you?" We don't realize how many people are really ready to accept Christ, if only someone would show them how. Our philosophy of witnessing should not be, "I'm sure he'll say 'no' to Jesus," but rather, "Who could say 'no' to Jesus?" We should always presuppose a positive response.

One day over lunch I was telling a friend how hungry people are to know the Lord. "That hasn't been my experience," he replied.

Just then the waiter came, and I mentioned to him, "You know, we're talking about how everyone wants to know the Lord. I'll bet you'd like to know the Lord, wouldn't you?"

"I sure would!" the waiter exclaimed.

My friend almost fell out of his chair. He knew I couldn't have pre-arranged this response because it was my first time in his city. The Lord just wanted to bring a waiter into His kingdom that day, and He wanted my friend to realize that people are hungry for the gospel, if only someone will show them how to receive Christ.

Had I not pre-supposed a positive response, I might not have had the courage to say what I did to the waiter.

I may have passed up the opportunity out of fear that the waiter would say "no" and I'd be embarrassed.

One of the most effective witnesses for Christ I have ever known was Arthur DeMoss. Art never was out to get a "spiritual scalp" just so he could tell people he had led someone to the Lord; this businessman let God's Spirit fill him and he always reached out in genuine love. And Art always pre-supposed a positive response.

We were having dinner together one evening in Mexico when the maitre d' came over to inquire about the food. Art smiled and said, "We're enjoying it very much. Now I'd like to ask *you* a question: Are you a Christian?"

The maitre d' shook his head. "No, I'm not."

"Would you like to be?"

"Why, yes, I would."

"Let me tell you how you can become a Christian," Art offered. And he led the maitre d' to the Lord right at our table. The guy was really excited about his new relationship with Jesus Christ.

Because Art DeMoss always pre-supposed a positive response, he didn't hesitate to witness for Christ at every opportunity. Individually and in large groups, Art introduced thousands of individuals to Jesus. Although he is now with the Lord, his beloved wife Nancy and the Arthur S. DeMoss Foundation continue to help spread the gospel throughout the world.

BARRIER 3: LACK OF PRACTICAL "KNOW-HOW"

"What do I say?"
"What scripture verses do I use?"
"How do I begin a conversation about Jesus?"
"How do I respond to questions or arguments?"
"How can I be sure he understands?"
"How do I encourage a decision?"
As a result of thousands of surveys, we have found

that the vast majority of Christians today not only believe they *should* share their faith; they really *want* to share their faith. Many Christians hear repeated messages from the pulpit that they should be "taking Christ to the marketplace" but they don't receive the practical, hands-on training that will ease their fears and help them witness effectively. The result is a guilt trip: They know they should, but they hesitate because they don't know how.

I am encouraged as I see more and more pastors providing evangelism training to their laypeople. There are many excellent training programs available to churches today. To become effective, you don't need a seminary degree or endless drills that prepare you for every conceivable situation. Within a couple of hours, you can learn a method of sharing Christ that has proven effective for millions of Christians around the world.

Thousands of pastors have taken this training, as have students and laypeople, who in turn have used it to witness to their loved ones, friends, neighbors, and casual acquaintances. We have hundreds of stories on file of people who received Christ through this presentation, then went out and led someone else to the Lord within forty-eight hours. It's simple, effective, and transferable.

We don't claim that it's the only way to share the gospel, or even the best way; but it is one method that works. In chapter 9, I'll walk you through the presentation step by step, just as if you are in one of our special training conferences. This book can be your training ground to help you gain the practical "know-how" of sharing your faith with confidence.

SUMMARY

●Three common barriers prevent Christians from witnessing without fear: (1) spiritual lethargy; (2) believing the enemy's "lines"; and (3) lack of practical know-how.

●You can conquer lethargy through "Spiritual Breathing." Confess sin (exhale), and appropriate God's cleansing, control and power (inhale).

●Satan has several favorite "lines" to keep you from sharing Christ with others. But since you are a member of God's kingdom, you need not yield to the enemy's deceit.

●Many well-intentioned Christians try to witness to others but get confused because they lack the practical know-how. In this book you'll learn a method that has proven successful in millions of diverse situations.

FOR REFLECTION AND ACTION

1. What are some of the reasons you may have been hesitant to witness to others in the past? Be specific.

2. Have you allowed distractions, lethargy, materialism, or unconfessed sin to rob you of your excitement in Christ? In what ways?

3. In a time of quiet prayer, ask God to reveal to you any unconfessed sin in your life. Take the steps to confess any such sin, and appropriate God's cleansing and forgiveness.

4. Resolve that, with the Lord's help, you won't allow the resistance from Satan to impede you as you reach out to others with the message of God's love and forgiveness.

*Understanding success and failure
can free you from the fear
of being "rejected"*

❧ 5 ❧

CONQUERING THE FEAR
OF FAILURE

O n a bright, hot day in Oklahoma many years
ago, I had concluded a visit with my parents
and was driving toward the airport in a rented
car. Ahead, I saw a big truck pulling out from a side
road, preparing to enter my lane of the highway.

In a flash of a moment, I thought, *I have the right
of way—surely, he's going to stop till I've gone past.* I
was wrong. He pulled right in front of me, and there
was no way I could stop or swerve to avoid him.

The crash totaled my car. My only injury was a
small scratch on my arm where my watch had moved.
But the truck driver, at fault for not yielding the right-
of-way, was so scared he almost had a nervous break-
down. We left the car beside the road, and the driver
drove me back to Coweta to see his boss.

The boss was the county commissioner, a long-time
friend of my family, to whom I had witnessed several
times previously with no results. He helped me handle
the details and reporting of the accident, then drove
me to the airport.

I just knew in my heart that the Lord would use these otherwise traumatic circumstances to allow me to share Christ again with this man. I decided to be straightforward with him.

"You know, I think the Lord may have allowed all this to happen so I could talk to you again. We just never know when an accident like that can take our lives. I was ready to go— suppose it had happened to you? Are you ready to go?"

But he still wasn't ready. "It just isn't for me," he said.

I got on the plane thankful that God had spared my life, but also sorrowful that, once again, this man had rejected the Lord Jesus Christ . . .

Failure. Fear of it can be one of the biggest cripplers of a faithful witness, for none of us likes to be "turned down." We tend to take it personally, regarding a rejection of our message as a rejection of our person. It hurts to be turned down.

It hurts even more when we've reached out in genuine love and we see the person refuse the greatest Gift ever offered to mankind, God's Son. Compassion for the lost does not come without tears.

But one of the liberating facts of the Christian life is that God does not ask anything of us which His Son has not already gone through Himself. Jesus Christ, to whom crowds walked miles for teaching and healing, saw His message rejected by many. Unlike us, however, Jesus did not grieve because His ego had been hurt. He grieved because people rejected the Giver of life and the gift of eternal life.

DID JESUS "FAIL" IN HIS WITNESSING?

Our Lord's ministry raises some interesting questions: Did He "fail" in His witnessing? Did He fail when the rich young ruler walked away from Him, refusing to give God first place in his life? Did He fail because

Judas Iscariot never received Him as his Messiah? Did He fail because one of the thieves crucified with Him refused to acknowledge His lordship? Was He a failure because many in the throngs around Him didn't receive Him?

Our Lord Himself answered these questions in His prayer to His heavenly Father at the end of His earthly ministry:

> "I brought glory to you here on earth by doing *everything* you told me to" (John 17:4, TLB).

Despite rejection, or what we might call "failures," our Lord Jesus Christ knew His mission was near completion. He had obeyed His Father's commission. He had brought the message, and was about to complete it with His death and resurrection. While He grieved over those who had rejected Him, He had not failed. He had done "everything" which God had given Him to do.

ALL HE ASKS IS THAT WE OBEY

Our heavenly Father asks no more of us than this: that we obey His command to "Go, and preach the gospel to every creature..." His command is not to "convert everyone." Jesus did not, and neither can we. But we can obey; we can spread the message to all who will listen and trust God for the results.

The ministry of Jesus Christ modeled for us a liberating truth about our witnessing efforts:

> *Success in witnessing is simply taking the initiative to share Christ in the power of the Holy Spirit, and leaving the results to God.*

Jesus never failed in His ministry. He accomplished all His Father had commissioned Him to do. Likewise, we do not fail if we obey what God wants us to do, motivated by genuine love and compassion.

We fail in witnessing only if we disobey God's command to share His love in the power of the Holy Spirit:

Failure in witnessing = failing to witness.

Had I not learned this truth, I would have been confused and defeated after that county commissioner rejected my message. Or I might have been discouraged one night in the parking lot in Washington, D.C., as I talked with the lot attendant about the Lord. I had just come from an exciting day on Capitol Hill, where I'd met with several national leaders for prayer and fellowship, and I sensed the Holy Spirit prompting me to ask the parking lot attendant if he was a Christian.

"My dad was a minister," he snapped, "and he didn't practice what he preached. So I had as much of that stuff as I could stand." He went on to tell how he had left the church and didn't want anything to do with God.

I couldn't help but get a lump in my throat as I thought of my own two sons: What if I had been inconsistent in my life and ministry? What if they had rejected God because of me?

We talked further. He had never received the Lord, and no matter what I said, he didn't want to do so now.

I went to my room in the hotel. But my soul wouldn't rest. Some may think, *He was just a parking lot attendant.* But this man was important to the Lord, and to me—just as important as the senators and government officials I had shared with earlier. And my heart went out to him. He had come so close to a life with Christ but had never embraced Him. I decided to go back downstairs, out into the parking lot, and talk further with him. But again he refused to receive Christ.

I hurt for him. His rejection of the Savior grieved me.

But had I failed?

If Christ's example is reliable, the task at hand

was not to get results. That may or may not happen. The task to which God had called me at that moment was to obey Him and share Christ as effectively and lovingly as I knew how.

NO-FAIL WITNESSING

When you obey God, motivated by love, you cannot fail. Your message might be accepted or rejected, but when you share Christ in obedience to God's command and the Holy Spirit's leading, you *succeed* in witnessing, no matter what the immediate result.

Success in witnessing is simply taking the initiative to share Christ in the power of the Holy Spirit, and leaving the results to God.

Read that statement aloud. Memorize it. Whenever the fear of failure begins to immobilize you from obeying God in witnessing, repeat this statement to yourself. Success in witnessing is simply sharing Christ in the power of the Holy Spirit, and leaving the results to God.

This is not to be interpreted as advocating a "hit-and-run" approach to witnessing and ministry, without conscientious follow-up to help new believers get into God's Word and grow in their faith. We firmly believe in the importance of a new Christian getting involved in (1) a church where our Lord is honored and the Word of God is proclaimed; and (2) systematic training in assurance of salvation, prayer, Bible study, fellowship with others and Christian growth.

REMOVING THE BURDEN OF "RESULTS"

Rather, this definition is intended to remove from today's frustrated Christian the burden of "results." To the faithful witness, there will come many joyous experiences of leading others to Christ. In most countries and cultures, we find that between 25 and 50 percent of those who hear the gospel (when presented by properly trained, Spirit-filled believers) receive Christ as a result. But if these positive numbers are true, then between 50 and 75 percent will say "no," at least upon first hearing.

Do the "no's" constitute failure? Go back to the definitions of success and failure in witnessing. Repeat them aloud. Do these percentages justify our not sharing Christ, because we might hit a streak of "no's"?

Once I was at Wheaton College in Wheaton, Illinois, holding a lay institute where we gave training in how to share one's faith. Part of the institute consisted of an afternoon of actual witnessing, door-to-door.

A good friend of mine, a professor at the college, came up to me and said, "I want to go with you, Bill. You're the professional."

"Look," I replied, "there are no professionals. Unless God works in the hearts of men, nothing happens. He only asks us to be obedient and proclaim the message."

Well, my friend thought that since I had taught many Christians how to witness more effectively, perhaps some of the "magic" would rub off on him. And I don't know why the Lord allowed it, but that day was absolutely the worst witnessing experience I've ever had. We were almost bodily thrown out of one house. Another listener reacted very angrily. We didn't see one single person who was interested in even talking with us. We hit an incredible, unexplainable streak of "no's" all afternoon.

In almost forty years of sharing my faith, I can count on the fingers of one hand the number of hostile rejections that I remember. But a good portion of them seemed to hit all at once on that day!

But, if anything good came of it, the experience made my friend feel better. Maybe God wanted to encourage him by illustrating that even Bill Bright, the supposed "professional" at witnessing—didn't have any power to lead anyone to the Lord unless God Himself did it.

WHAT CHRIST TAUGHT ABOUT FAILURE

For those who question whether we should even try, considering the chance that a number of listeners will say "no," there is assurance for us in the Parable of the Sower. Here, Christ illustrated the varied effectiveness of His message:

"A farmer was sowing grain in his fields. As he scattered the seed across the ground, some fell beside a path, and the birds came and ate it. And some fell on rocky soil where there was little depth of earth; the plants sprang up quickly enough in the shallow soil, but the hot sun soon scorched them and they withered and died, for they had so little root. Other seeds fell among thorns, and the thorns choked out the tender blades.

"But some fell on good soil, and produced a crop that was thirty, sixty, and even a hundred times as much as he had planted" (Matthew 13:3-8, TLB).

There are four types of listeners, Christ taught. And only one of the four will take the message (the seed) and put it to work in his life.

"The good ground represents the heart of a man who listens to the message and understands it and goes out and brings thirty, sixty, or even a hundred others into the Kingdom" (Matthew 13:23, TLB).

The other three listeners (types of soil) will squander the message or reject it outright. Jesus Christ Himself recognized that, and though His compassion drove Him to love and long for every human soul, He knew that man would exercise his God-given power of free choice both for and against Him. And man continues to do so today.

WE JUST NEVER KNOW ...

So there will be "no's." As we discussed in the previous chapter, we should always pre-suppose a positive response, since the world is hungrier now for the gospel than ever before. Indeed, the fields are white unto harvest. But when the "no's" come, we shouldn't be surprised or discouraged.

And we just never know, really, where the "no's" will lead.

In 1976, Tom and Dorrine, a married couple from Washington, D.C., went witnessing from their church as part of the "I found it!" Here's Life, America campaign. They visited a home where a man and woman, who were living together unmarried, were so loaded on drugs that they couldn't carry on a conversation.

So Tom and Dorrine left a gospel booklet on the coffee table, and suggested that when the couple felt like it they could read the booklet. Tom and Dorrine had received their "no," unspoken yet unmistakable.

Two weeks later, the woman came across the booklet and began to read. Its simple gospel presentation convicted her, and she knelt in her living room and received Jesus Christ into her life. Then she gave it to the man she'd been living with, and after several days he pulled out the booklet, read through it, and accepted the Lord.

Several weeks passed, and this couple listened to Christian programs on radio and TV. As they heard more of God's Word, they wanted to attend church, and one Sunday they entered the church down the block. It was the same church from which my friends had gone witnessing.

When the pastor gave the invitation, the man and woman went forward to declare their new faith in God and to be baptized. They ceased living together as singles, but soon were married. Five years later, they had grown so much in their walk with the Lord that he was asked to be a deacon in the church and she was active in several ministries.

When Tom and Dorrine left the haze of this couple's drug-filled living room that first day, they must have thought, *Boy, what a waste of time!*

But because of that initial contact, made out of obedience to a God who says, "Go, and preach the gospel," God turned this couple's "no" into a "yes" and brought two new dedicated believers into His kingdom.

There really is no wasted witness.

THE LONG LETTER

Another "no" that stands out in my memory is a long letter I wrote to a nationally known sales consultant. I had met him at a conference where he was the featured speaker, and we struck up conversation and enjoyed a good visit together.

I did share Christ with him, and he seemed interested but was noncommittal. "Why don't you drop me a line with some more information?" he said to me as we parted company.

I went back to my office and thought and prayed hard about what I would write him. Over the next several days, I felt the Lord guiding me as I pulled together the key Scriptures and concepts of the plan of salvation into a letter to my new friend. I made a copy, mailed him the original, and prayed that God would use my effort in this man's life.

To my knowledge, this gentleman never did receive Christ into his life. He gave me an implied "no." But God was working in ways I never would have imagined.

As some trusted friends and I reviewed what I had written in the letter, they suggested that I print it in quantity, under a fictitious salutation, as a witnessing tool. I addressed the letter to a Dr. Van Dusen (I thought he sounded like an intriguing sort) and we printed several thousand copies. Over the years, the Van Dusen letter has been reprinted many times to meet the demand of our staff, Christian businessmen, and other lay men and women who have used it to lead thousands of men and women to the Lord.

THE PHONE CALL

One evening during our family dinner time, I received a long distance phone call. The woman on the other end of the line told me of a printed letter to a "Dr. Van Dusen" she had found in the seat of a commercial airliner.

"Are you the Bill Bright who wrote this letter?" she asked. She proceeded to ask me some questions, then said, "I would like to become a Christian. Can you help me?"

What a thrill it was to lead this sincere woman in prayer over the phone as she received Christ as her Savior and Lord. But it didn't stop there.

In the family room with her were five other family members and friends. Each of them had read the Van Dusen letter. One by one, each of them came to the phone and, after some questions and discussion, received Christ.

There really is no wasted witness.

We fail in witnessing only if we fail to witness.

Success in witnessing is simply sharing Christ in the power of the Holy Spirit, and leaving the results to God.

. . . It had been many years since my car accident in Oklahoma, and Vonette's father passed away. We returned to Oklahoma and were at the graveside service at the cemetery when the presiding pastor gave a challenge to the people standing there.

"Now, Roy Zachary was ready to meet the Lord," he said. "Are you? If you're not ready, Christ wants to come into your life."

I turned around, and behind me stood my county commissioner friend from years before. I could see tears forming in the corners of his eyes.

The last thing I wanted to do was disturb the sacredness of the moment. But I knew that, again, God was nudging me to speak with him.

"Are you ready, my friend? Don't you think it's about time you make this decision?"

"Yes, sir," his voice cracked as he whispered. "It's time." And when the service ended, we moved to a private spot and he received Christ through a prayer that began:

"Lord Jesus, I need you . . ."

Isn't it great that we can leave the results to God?

SUMMARY

●Success in witnessing is simply taking the initiative to share Christ in the power of the Holy Spirit, and leaving the results to God.

●Failure in witnessing is failing to witness.

●God does not hold us accountable for results—only for our obedience or lack of obedience.

●Quite often, a sharing opportunity which we might deem a "failure" will be used by God in the future to bring that person to Himself. Thus, even if we do not happen to see immediate results, we can plant a positive seed in the person's life and trust God to bring forth fruit.

FOR REFLECTION AND ACTION

1. Up to this point in your life, how have you defined success in witnessing? Failure in witnessing? Have you allowed your definitions to prevent you from sharing Christ out of fear of rejection?

2. Memorize the definitions from this chapter of success and failure in witnessing.

3. Resolve that whenever you share your faith and don't see immediate results, you will not take it as personal rejection. Trust God to nurture the seed

you have planted, pray regularly for that person, and be obedient to the Lord's guidance in future contacts with the individual.

❧ 6 ❧

HOW TO PRAY FOR YOUR FRIENDS & LOVED ONES

She was in her mid-fifties, and as she came up to me following a lecture her eyes were red from weeping. "Our son is almost thirty," she began, her voice trembling, "and he is still living a rebellious life. I don't think he's a Christian and I don't know how to get through to him."

This woman's story was like hundreds I hear every year from concerned fellow believers: A family member, a neighbor, a friend or co-worker needs Christ. The concerned believer has been praying for that person—sometimes for years—without an apparent answer to the prayers.

I'm sure that must have been the feeling my mother had as she prayed for her children and for my father. Mother and Dad were married thirty years before Dad received Christ. Their love for each other was strong, but Dad's indifference to the Lord must have caused my mother to shed many tears. But she kept praying—for him, and for my brothers and sisters and me—until finally, thirty years later, her prayers began to see results and eventually our entire family received the Lord.

PRAYING FOR MY FIANCÉE

I must confess I struggled through many tough prayer sessions over my fiancée, Vonette, during our engagement in the late 1940s.

Vonette was attractive, personable, and came from a fine family. Although we had been friends during our growing-up years, it wasn't until I received Christ in Southern California that our friendship blossomed into romantic love and eventually engagement. Vonette had always been very active in her church, so I assumed she was a vital Christian. Soon, however, I began to wonder about her commitment to Christ.

On the night I had proposed to her, I told her, "I love you, Vonette, and look forward to spending our life together. And I know you'll understand that God will always come first in my life, and in our marriage."

She didn't say anything at the time. I repeated this commitment several months later, during my stopover in Coweta enroute to Princeton Theological Seminary. This time she spoke up. "I'm not sure that's right," she bristled. "I think a man's family should be his first concern."

I started to argue, but dropped it, knowing we would have plenty of time to work things out. In the fall of 1947, I enrolled in the first class at Fuller Theological Seminary in California to be closer to my business. As I worked toward my degree at Fuller, Vonette's personal relationship with Christ continued to trouble me.

WHY HADN'T GOD ANSWERED MY PRAYERS?

Was it true, as I had originally thought, that God had chosen Vonette to be my wife? If so, why hadn't He answered my prayers for her salvation? How could we possibly become "unequally yoked" and still be in

His will? How could she possibly share my excitement and love for the Lord?

I had been so sure that Vonette was the one for me. I loved her, and she loved me. Yet, she simply could not accept the fact that her relationship with the Lord needed to go beyond mere church activity and become a whole-hearted commitment of her life to Jesus Christ.

It was a tough, emotional time for both of us. *Lord, I remember praying almost every day, I believe You brought Vonette into my life. I love her, and want to marry her, but I know it is not Your will for a believer to marry an unbeliever. Please, Father, help Vonette to trust You with her life.*

Upon Vonette's graduation with a home economics degree, I suggested she visit her brother, who lived in Southern California. She thought this might be a good idea, a kind of "last chance" time for our relationship when we would decide either yes or no. Vonette confided to a friend, "I am either going to rescue Bill from this religious fanaticism or come back without a ring."

FEELING INADEQUATE TO SHARE

During her visit, Vonette went with me to a meeting of several hundred Christian college students at Forest Home Christian Conference Center. Although I had been learning to introduce others to Christ, I felt very inadequate in talking to Vonette about Him. I was fearful that she might go through the motions of accepting Christ because of our relationship, but not really experience a change in her life. So I hoped I could get her to talk with someone more able and objective than I.

Perhaps if she could meet with Dr. Henrietta Mears, who had been so instrumental in my conversion, she would see the validity of a personal relationship with Christ. In addition to being director of Christian education at Hollywood Presbyterian Church, Dr. Mears had founded Forest Home and was scheduled to be there during this conference.

Just as I had been positively impressed at that Christian movie star's barn party a few years before, Vonette was impressed by the many vibrant, happy young people at the conference. She liked the quality of life they possessed, but was skeptical about their depth. After a couple of days, she concluded that they were so enthusiastic about Christianity because it was so new to them—their excitement would wear off. After all, she had been reared in the church and didn't see anything to get excited about.

"THIS JUST ISN'T FOR ME . . ."

"Bill," she told me one evening, "I respect your commitment, but this just isn't for me."

Her words hit me hard. I had prayed so fervently for her. I cared deeply for her, romantically and spiritually. I wanted her to experience the joy of a personal walk with the Lord. But she was rejecting Him, and in so doing, it seemed that she was rejecting me.

"Are you sure?" I asked.

"I'm sure," Vonette whispered, her voice choking. "I just don't think all this personal relationship talk is real—or necessary. But I can see that it's important to you, and—"

Tears came to her eyes as she struggled for words. I could feel my heart pounding as I sensed what was coming.

"—and it's built a barrier between us. Maybe it would be best for us to call off our engagement."

A lump welled up in my throat as I realized what was happening. I wanted her for my wife, but spiritually we were worlds apart. I could not give up my faith, and she could not subscribe to it. Why hadn't God answered my prayers for her?

I took both her hands in mine and looked directly into her moist eyes. "Vonette, you told me you respect my commitment. I also respect you for the way you've weighed this carefully. Before we make a final decision, would you do one more thing?"

"What?"

"Talk with Dr. Mears. I think you'll like her. She has an inquiring, scientific mind like you do. She can explain these truths much better than I can."

A VISIT WITH DR. MEARS

Hesitantly, Vonette agreed. The next morning she entered Dr. Mears' cottage with the attitude that *It won't do any good, but I want Bill to know I tried everything possible.* And while Dr. Mears and Vonette talked, I paced back and forth outside the cottage, praying my heart out.

Time dragged. Fifteen minutes. A half hour. *Lord Jesus, break through to her . . .*

Forty-five minutes. An hour. *Father, open Vonette's heart to You . . .*

Ninety minutes. Suddenly the door burst open, and Vonette came bounding into my arms. Tears of joy streaked her face and her smile could have replaced the sun. She didn't have to say a word—I knew what had happened, and tears of gratitude filled my eyes, too.

God had indeed answered my prayers. Not according to my timetable, but in a way that glorified Him and confirmed His will for our life together. Several years later, Vonette recalled in writing what took place during her visit with Dr. Mears:

> Dr. Mears was one of the most vibrant, enthusiastic personalities I had ever met. She was waiting for me, and the entire conference staff, without my knowledge, had been praying for my conversion. Dr. Mears explained that she had taught chemistry in Minneapolis, and that she could understand how I was thinking. (I had minored in chemistry in college, and everything had to be practical and workable to me. This was one of the reasons I had questioned the validity of Christianity.)
>
> As she explained simply to me from God's Word

how I could be sure I knew God, she used terminology very familiar to me. She explained that, just as a person going into a chemistry laboratory experiment follows the table of chemical valence, so it is possible for a person to enter God's spiritual laboratory and follow His formula of knowing and following Him.

During the next hour, she lovingly proceeded to explain to me who Christ is and how I could know Him personally. "Dr. Mears," I said, "if Jesus Christ is the way, then how do I meet Him?"

Dr. Mears responded, "In Revelation 3:20 Christ says, 'Behold, I stand at the door and knock; if any one hears My voice and opens the door, I will come in to him, and will dine with him, and he with Me.' Receiving Christ is simply a matter of turning your life—your will, your emotions, your intellect— completely over to Him. John 1:12 says, 'But as many as received Him, to them He gave the right to become children of God, even to those who believe in His name.' "

When Dr. Mears finished, I thought, *If what she tells me is absolutely true, I have nothing to lose and everything to gain.* I bowed my head and prayed, asking Christ to come into my heart. And at that moment, as I look back, my life began to change.

God became a reality in my life. For the first time I was ready to trust Him. I became aware that my prayers were getting beyond the ceiling. No longer did I have to *try* to love people—there just seemed to be a love that flowed from within that I did not have to create.

God had added a new dimension to my life, and I found myself becoming as enthusiastic as Bill, Dr. Mears and the other students—and as eager as they to share Christ with others.

I have prayed intensively for hundreds of others over the years and, while many have received Christ, others still have not. So I can readily identify with the concerned believer whose heart aches for the salvation of a friend or loved one. From my personal experience and study of God's Word, I can assure you that the key starting point in bringing a loved one to Christ is prayer.

GOD IS NOT WILLING THAT ANY SHOULD PERISH

Just as Jesus prayed that the Holy Spirit would do a work in the lives of His disciples, so we can pray that the Holy Spirit would convict a non-believer and give him a strong desire for the ways of God. God's Word assures us that "God is not willing that any should perish, but that all would come to repentance" (2 Peter 3:9). God desires the soul of your loved one, friend or neighbor even more than you do.

Sometimes, however, in His mysterious, sovereign timing, He chooses to wait for the prayers of a concerned believer to unleash the Holy Spirit in that person's heart. As someone has said, "Prayer is not conquering God's reluctance but laying hold of God's willingness."

But why does He sometimes seem to take so long to answer our prayers? Why does He allow an unsaved person to continue in darkness when our prayers are so urgent?

FIVE REASONS WHY YOUR PRAYERS MAY NOT BE ANSWERED

Let's look at five important reasons why your prayers for friends and loved ones may not be answered according to your desires. Then we'll discuss five positive steps to take in order to be sure your prayers are effective.

1. You may not be on "praying ground."

There may be unconfessed sin in your life. Psalm 66:18 tells us that "If I regard iniquity in my heart, the Lord will not hear me." It sounds harsh, but it's a basic law of man's relationship with God. If we have climbed back up on the throne of our lives through unconfessed sin (unscriptural attitudes or actions, or disobedience) we have moved out of fellowship with

God. He is still in our lives, but He waits for us to restore fellowship (remember, He has given us freedom to choose). He does not hear the prayer of the person who holds unconfessed sin in his heart, unless it is a prayer of confession.

2. You may be praying in unbelief.

Many Christians beg and plead with God, praying passionately almost every day, but as time passes their faith in God's miracles dwindles. They may even be fooled into thinking that God has not chosen their loved one for His kingdom. Such thinking can cause confusion, weariness in prayer, and even rebellion on the part of the believer.

3. Your lifestyle might be a negative witness.

Without realizing it, the praying believer might himself be a hindrance to the salvation of a loved one. Prayerfully, honestly examine yourself:

●Are you inconsistent in your personal walk with the Lord?

●Do you often speak negatively of others, or look on life in general with a negative spirit?

●Have you wronged your friend in any way, and failed to ask forgiveness and make restitution?

●Do you fail to handle your personal finances responsibly, paying your bills late or making unwise decisions?

●Do you fail to keep your property in good shape? Dress and groom neatly?

●Do you tearfully nag and plead with your loved one about spiritual things? Or is your relationship a loving, positive one?

●Does your life reflect a legalistic, self-righteous Christianity? Or do you present a positive, scriptural model for others to see?

4. You may not be obeying God's leading in witnessing opportunities.

Many Christians pray fervently for an unbelieving friend or loved one, yet pass up countless opportunities to present the gospel directly to that person. One gentleman told me, "I'm praying hard for a friend of ours. We're together often, but I don't want to say anything—he might think I'm pressuring him and it might ruin any chance of his receiving Christ in the future."

Instead of rightly considering times together a divine appointment, he—like many well-meaning Christians today—was hoping that his friend might absorb Christianity by osmosis. Or, that someone else, somewhere, someday, would lead his friend to Christ. It could well be that God was tapping him to be the bearer of good news to his friend, but he was disregarding God's leading.

If you are in a similar situation, consider: What is really the most loving thing to do? Share with your friend a direct, logical presentation of the gospel . . . or hope that maybe someday your friend might become a Christian on his own?

5. God's sovereign timing may not be the same as yours.

This can be the toughest reason to comprehend, for human logic would seem to dictate that God would want our friends and loved ones to enter His kingdom just as quickly as possible. However, for reasons only God can explain, His timing is different from ours. I wanted Vonette to receive Him the moment I first told her of my own decision for Christ. I wanted my Dad to accept Christ on that first visit to Coweta. But, despite my intensive prayers, God chose a different timetable.

HOW TO PRAY FOR YOUR FRIENDS AND LOVED ONES

God commands us to pray without ceasing and to

devote ourselves to prayer (1 Thessalonians 5:17 and Colossians 4:2). Prayer is foundational to our spiritual vitality and to our ongoing witness for Christ. As Louis Evans, Jr., wrote, "The man who kneels to God can stand up to anything."

Through the energizing of God's Holy Spirit, you can turn those five reasons for unanswered prayer into five stepping stones of faith. As you pray for your friends, loved ones, neighbors and co-workers:

1. Be sure you are a Christian, and that there is no unconfessed sin in your life.

Have you actually received Jesus Christ as your own personal Savior and Lord? This, of course, is the first step. By inviting Him to take control of your life, you can be assured that He is indeed in your life and that you have moved from the kingdom of darkness to the kingdom of light.

Then, since God does not hear the prayer of a sinful heart, it is vital that you apply the principles of "Spiritual Breathing" moment by moment, day by day. Study appendices B and C to be sure you understand how to "exhale the impure" (confess sin) and "inhale the pure" (appropriate God's promised forgiveness and cleansing). As you breathe spiritually, fellowship with God is restored, and your prayers will be heard.

2. Pray in faith, believing God will do the work you're asking Him to do.

I led the tearful mother whose story began this chapter, along with a friend of hers, into a quiet room away from the crowd. We talked a few moments about her prayers for her wayward son, and it soon became apparent that perhaps the way she was praying was part of the problem.

"I've prayed every day," she wept. "I pray without ceasing. I've pleaded with God every single day to turn Jack around . . ."

She buried her face in her hands, sobbing, as her

friend put a caring arm around her.

"Mary," I began, "let me ask you a question. Do you believe God wants Jack to become a Christian?"

Mary's face shot up from her hands, her eyes wide in disbelief. "Of *course* I do," she sobbed. She pulled a Kleenex from her purse and dabbed at her eyes.

"I know you do," I assured her. "But are you praying scripturally?"

She sniffled, and turned the Kleenex in her hands to find a dry spot of tissue. "Yes. I pray without ceasing."

"Mary, there's more to it than that. But let's back up a moment to get some reassurance from God's Word. First, we can personalize John 3:16: 'For God so loved Jack that He gave His only Son, that if Jack believes in Him, he will have eternal life.'

"Let's also personalize 2 Peter 3:9: 'God is not willing that anyone (including Jack) perish, but for all (*all* includes Jack) to come to repentance.' And 1 Timothy 2:4: 'God our Savior desires all men (*all men* includes Jack) to be saved and to come to the knowledge of the truth.' Mary, do you believe that? Do you claim those promises for Jack?"

"Yes."

"God wants Jack to turn around even more than we do. Jack's salvation, then, is God's will. Do you believe that?"

For the first time, I saw a hint of a smile tugging at the corner of her quivering mouth. "Yes, I do."

"Good. Now 1 John 5:14 and 15 teaches that if we ask anything according to God's will, He hears us and answers us. Let's ask ourselves again: Is it God's will that Jack come to Christ? Is He not willing that any should perish?"

Her smile grew as she began to see the promise of Scripture. "It's God's will that Jack turn around," she stated resolutely.

"And if you pray according to God's will?"

"God will hear me, and answer me."

"Does it matter how you feel emotionally?"

"No. He'll answer me."

"Will it always be according to your timetable?"

"No."

"So on what basis can you claim and look forward to Jack's commitment to Christ?"

"The fact that God's Word is reliable?"

"That's right!" I encouraged. "So let's covenant together for prayer, on the authority of Scripture, that *by faith in God's Word* we claim Jack for God's kingdom."

Together, Mary, her friend and I prayed, asking God to change Jack's heart and to lead him into a decision for Christ. When we were through with the prayer, I had one more important thought for her.

"Now, Mary, let me ask you another question—and this leads to what I was saying about praying scripturally. If you were God, would you want someone to continually beg and plead, day in and day out, for something you had already promised? Or would you rather have that person ask for it once, and from then on simply say, 'Thank You that You are going to answer according to Your promise in Scripture'?"

"I—I think the continual begging and pleading would be an insult."

"I think so too, Mary. The Bible says that without faith it is impossible to please God, and that whatever is without faith is sin. Now there's nothing wrong with tears—in fact, we are admonished to shed tears for the lost. And there are times when we should be praying our hearts out. But God wants us to pray in faith, trusting Him to answer according to His promises."

Mary and her friend left that day with their burden lifted. They had determined to trust God to change Jack. Almost two years later, I received a letter from her announcing that Jack had committed his life to Jesus Christ and was a changed man.

Are you eager to see your friends and loved ones receive Christ? Then begin today to pray in faith.

Successful praying is simply asking God to work according to His promised will, and leaving the results to Him.

Make a list of all for whom you're praying. Keep a prayer journal and make notes of special things that happen to them as time passes. Ask God once for the salvation of each friend and loved one, and realize the liberating truth that God loves them even more than you do. Thereafter, pray regularly, thanking God in faith that they will become Christians.

3. Be sure your lifestyle reflects Jesus Christ.

"How can we be sure that we belong to him?" 1 John asks. "By looking within ourselves: are we really trying to do what he wants us to do?" (1 John 2:3, TLB).

If any of the lifestyle questions asked earlier describe your life, or if the Holy Spirit points out other areas where your words, actions or attitudes are inconsistent with your walk with the Lord, ask God to change those negative patterns. "Walking in the Spirit" means allowing the Spirit of the Lord to infuse you with the attributes of Jesus Christ.

Ask God to make you loving, positive, honest and caring in all aspects of your life. Ask Him to remind you quickly when you slip into a behavioral pattern that presents a negative witness. (See appendix C, "How to Walk in the Spirit," for helpful instruction in this important area.)

4. Share Christ verbally, as opportunities arise.

Someone has said, "Prayer is not an argument with God to persuade Him to move things our way, but an exercise by which we are enabled by His Spirit to move ourselves His way." In praying for the salvation of friends and loved ones, this quite often is the case. Our prayer for others prompts and enables us to give verbal witness to that very person, if only we obey God's prompting.

Could it be that God has not yet answered your prayer because you have not been willing to be the bearer of His message? You have in your possession the most joyful news ever announced. You have been praying urgently for this person. Is there any scriptural reason why you shouldn't make the good news clear to your friend or loved one?

The next time you're alone with this person, consider it a divine appointment—an opportunity God has brought specifically to you to share the gospel with confidence. Remember: Success in witnessing is simply taking the initiative to share Christ in the power of the Holy Spirit, and leaving the results to God.

5. Trust in God's timing.

Your friend or loved one may surprise you, and eagerly accept Christ as Savior upon first hearing. Or, he or she may not respond at first opportunity. Continue to pray, thanking God in faith that He will answer according to His expressed will. Continue fellowship with the person, to show that you love him unconditionally. Conscientiously model the positive, victorious Christian life through your attitudes, actions and words. As the Lord leads, talk about Jesus again in your conversations, without hesitancy or embarrassment.

You have planted the seed. God, if His promises are true, will harvest that seed in His sovereign timing. He may use you, He may use someone else, or He may bring your loved one to Himself in a special way. So keep praying, loving, and trusting.

THE DAILY FOUNDATION

Make prayer a daily foundation to your faith in Jesus Christ. Do not make the mistake of praying simply for your own personal intimacy with the Savior, or for the endless lists of "things" we always ask God for. We must pray daily for the souls of our friends and loved ones, asking God what role He would have us play in their exposure to His plan for their lives.

Likewise, we must be in a constant attitude of prayer for those we might encounter on a casual basis, realizing that God wants us to proclaim the good news to all who will listen. As we pray for the Holy Spirit's wisdom and power, and for the open minds and hearts of the listeners, God will truly bless our efforts to share His goodness with them.

SUMMARY

●God is not willing that any should perish. This includes special friends and loved ones for whom you have been praying for years.

●It is God's will that your friends and loved ones receive Him. However, His will does not operate according to your timetable.

●There are five reasons why your prayers may not be answered: (1) You may have unconfessed sin in your life; (2) You may be praying in unbelief; (3) Your lifestyle might be a negative witness; (4) You may not be obeying God's leading in witnessing opportunities; (5) God's sovereign timing may not be the same as yours.

●We are to pray in faith, believing that God will bring our loved ones to Himself. Pray once for their salvation; thereafter, thank God in faith that He will honor your request in His timing.

●Successful prayer is simply asking God to work according to His promised will, and leaving the results to Him.

FOR REFLECTION AND ACTION

1. Which special friends or loved ones have been on your heart recently? Have you ever felt that a particular situation was "hopeless"?

2. What principles have you learned from this chapter to help you in your prayer and witness to these

people? Think of each person by name and apply the principles you've learned to each situation.

3. Honestly consider the five suggested reasons why prayers may not be answered: (1) Is there unconfessed sin in your life? (2) Have you been praying in unbelief? (3) Is your lifestyle a negative witness? (4) Have you failed to obey God's leading in witnessing opportunities? (5) Are you expecting God to work according to your timetable?

Is the Holy Spirit revealing any problem areas in your life? Take the five steps recommended in this chapter to make sure your prayers will be unhindered.

4. Continue to pray without ceasing, but instead of begging and pleading with God, thank and praise Him by faith that He is going to answer your prayers in His perfect timing.

❧ 7 ❧

HOW TO GUIDE A CONVERSATION TOWARD JESUS

"**I** had a great opportunity to talk with someone about Christ today," a sharp young woman once told me, "but I just couldn't think of a way to begin. I felt very awkward. How do you guide a conversation toward Jesus, in a way that's natural and doesn't seem contrived?"

Some folks practically shout "Repent!" as if from some seedy street corner in the inner city.

Others inch their way ever so cautiously toward spiritual things—so cautiously, in fact, that the conversation never does get around to the Lord Jesus.

I'm not personally comfortable with the first approach. And I know from experience that the second can get so easily sidetracked that the gospel usually loses out to the weather, football, or stories of Johnny's latest escapades at school.

So there needs to be a happy medium—a means of turning a conversation toward Christ that is natural and sensitive, yet which helps the person you're talking with face his need for the Savior. In chapters 8 and 9

I'll show you a proven, highly focused gospel presentation you can use to introduce others to Christ. In this chapter, we'll examine effective ways to lead in to the gospel presentation.

Basically, the person you're talking with falls into one of two categories. Either he's (1) a loved one, friend, neighbor or co-worker, or he's (2) a casual encounter—someone next to you on a bus or plane, a waitress or cab driver, the person seated next to you at a concert or seminar, or a business contact.

FRIENDSHIP EVANGELISM VS. INITIATIVE EVANGELISM

For the person with whom you're in frequent contact, your approach should generally be less direct. It's important to take the time to build a relationship of friendship and trust, to show by word and deed that you love and care about him. This approach has been called "friendship evangelism" by some, and it does have its place. Especially important among family members, but also recommended for other close relationships, friendship evangelism urges a "go slow" approach that is intended to virtually love the non-Christian into God's kingdom.

But with its strengths also come two glaring weaknesses. First, many Christians mistakenly subscribe to the friendship evangelism philosophy to the extent that they rarely share the gospel with another because "our relationship isn't quite strong enough yet." Then, when they feel the relationship finally is strong, they are afraid to say anything that might spoil the friendship. To justify this approach, or non-approach, they decide they'll "wait for the non-believer to ask *me* about my personal faith," and try to simply model Christianity through their non-verbal witness. As a result, the gospel often falls by the wayside.

The second weakness of the friendship evangelism philosophy is that Christians can also use it as an excuse to never share their faith. Some Christian authors have written that "initiative evangelism" (sharing Christ with casual encounters, door-to-door canvassing, etc.) will almost invariably turn off the non-Christian because it cannot present Christ from a basis of friendship and relational trust.

Yet, we see initiative evangelism modeled for us throughout Scripture. Jesus had only a few moments with the Samaritan woman He met at the well, but He took the initiative to talk to her about Living Water. In Philip's brief encounter with the Ethiopian eunuch, he led the stranger to Christ. Paul wrote, "Everywhere we go we talk about Christ to all who will listen . . ." (Colossians 1:28, TLB).

As I have suggested, I believe there is a place for friendship evangelism, and I would be wrong to say that the philosophy of friendship evangelism is unscriptural. Likewise, those who hold that it is the only way to share Christ, and that initiative evangelism is unscriptural and ineffective, are just as wrong. A careful reading of the New Testament makes it emphatically clear that initiative evangelism is the intent of our Lord when He commands us to "Go into all the world, and preach the gospel to every creature."

Both approaches have their proper place in the task of spreading the gospel. But I am convinced that if I were to err in sharing Christ, the Lord would prefer that I err on the side of taking initiative than in not sharing Him at all.*

"LETUS": FIVE IMPORTANT STEPS

Let's look at five important steps for guiding a conversation toward Jesus. These will prove helpful whether you're sharing with a close acquaintance or a

---

*For a definitive examination of the issue of "friendship evangelism" vs. "initiative evangelism," see *Tell It Often, Tell It Well* by Mark McCloskey (Here's Life Publishers, 1986).

casual encounter. To help you remember them, utilize the acrostic, "LETUS."

L ove
E stablish rapport
T alk about Jesus
U se stories (if time allows)
S equence of questions

Love

Your motivation should be love, and the other person should see it in your eyes and facial expressions, hear it in your voice, and witness it in your attitudes and actions. If he senses that you're speaking to him out of obligation or to attain a spiritual trophy, he'll turn cold in a hurry. Paul wrote, "Let love be without hypocrisy" (Romans 12:9).

To help us obey that command, God promises in 1 John 5:14,15 that if we ask anything according to His will, He will hear and answer us. So, to be sure you are reaching out in genuine love, ask God for His love to flow through you.

The first listed fruit of the Spirit is love (Galatians 5:20). You can trust that as God controls you through His Holy Spirit, He will fill you with love for others. And you can communicate that love by taking sincere interest in the other person through friendly conversation, eye contact, a pleasant facial expression, and questions to keep the conversation going.

Establish rapport

Take the time to establish rapport. In some situations, it might be just a few moments—one brief comment or two to express friendliness. Other times, such as on an airplane or with an acquaintance, you may want to take more time to ask the other person about his vocation, interests, etc.

In training home visitation teams, we usually advise a visit of five minutes at the most before leading in to the gospel, since team members are unexpected guests in the person's home. Be sensitive to the surroundings and to the other person's time constraints.

Talk about Jesus

A common mistake among Christians who are beginning to share their faith is that they allow conversations to become sidetracked. It is generally best not to talk about religions, denominations, churches, and personalities. Many people have bitter remembrances—real or imagined—from their past about these peripheral issues. But if you stay focused on the person of Jesus Christ, your listener can't help but be attracted to Him.

A taxi driver in Australia said to me, "I gave up all religion in World War II. I want nothing to do with a God who allows people to kill each other."

"Wait a minute," I objected. "You are accusing God of something for which man is responsible. It's the evil in man— his sin—that causes him to hate and steal and kill."

I explained the difference between religion, which is man's search for God, and Christianity, which is God's revelation of Himself to man through Jesus Christ. As I focused on Jesus, the cab driver's whole attitude changed. After we reached our destination, he prayed with me, asking Christ to come into his life.

Use stories (if time allows)

The word *witness* literally means to give testimony of facts or events. In other words, to tell the true story of how Christ has changed your life, and the lives of others.

The New Testament Christians witnessed by telling stories of how Jesus Christ died and rose from the dead, how He changed their lives, and what He offered to everyone who would receive Him. Paul told of his dramatic conversion experience. Their witness through stories not only caught the attention of the listeners, but showed them vividly how they, too, could commit themselves to the Lord.

Stories are among the most effective methods of teaching. Think back to the most recent sermon you heard. Which do you remember best: the concept upon concept of the message, or the stories the pastor told to illustrate those concepts?

At Campus Crusade for Christ, we teach each of our new staff, and everyone who goes through our training conferences, to write out, polish and memorize a three-minute testimony. It is to cover three basic points: (1) What your life was like before you received Christ; (2) How you received Christ; and (3) What your life is like since you received Christ. We encourage everyone to be as specific as possible, humorous if appropriate, and very clear when explaining how they invited Christ into their lives (so that if the listener were to have no other opportunity, he would know from the three-minute testimony how he can receive Christ as Savior).

Let me strongly encourage you to write and memorize your own three-minute testimony. Practice delivering it conversationally, perhaps with a friend. You'll be surprised how often it will come in handy in speaking engagements and witnessing opportunities—and at how effective it can be in helping you move from casual conversation to the actual gospel.*

Sequence of questions

One of the most effective ways we've found to lead in to a discussion of the gospel is a sequence of directed questions. They can be used whether you have just a few minutes with someone or you've known that person for a lifetime.

The first group of questions I'll share with you is helpful to use after a non-Christian has attended a

---

*For samples of the three-minute testimony, see Vonette Bright's story in the previous chapter, Bill Armstrong's story in chapter 8, and appendix D.

Christian event (church service, lecture, concert, seminar) or if you have given the non-believer a Christian book, magazine or tape. After the event, or after the person has had a chance to read or listen to what you gave him, ask:

1. "What did you think of the concert?" (or church service, book, etc.)

2. "Did it make sense to you?"

3. "Have you made the wonderful discovery of knowing Christ personally?"

4. "You'd like to, wouldn't you?" Or, "Would you like to?"

Listen intently to the person's answer to each question, then ask the next one in the sequence. You'll see that each subsequent question is appropriate to ask no matter what answer was given to the preceding question. The fourth question provides a natural lead-in to the gospel presentation which you'll be learning in chapter 9.

We have taught thousands of Christian high school and college students and lay people to approach their friends with these questions following a Christian concert, drama series or other event. For example, after a performance by Andre Kole, the Christian illusionist, you might see dozens of clusters of young people throughout the auditorium as Christian students take the initiative to ask others, "What did you think of the performance? Did his comments about Jesus Christ make sense to you? Have you made the discovery of knowing Christ personally? You'd like to, wouldn't you?"

In the majority of cases, the person who answers "no" or "I'm not sure" to the third question will say "yes" or "perhaps" to the fourth. And the door is open for the gospel.

In the midst of a hectic cross-country speaking trip, I was seated between two enlisted men on a plane. Exhausted, I pulled out a copy of the Van Dusen letter for each of them and said, "Would you please read this while I take a quick nap? Then I'd like to find out what you think of it."

I dozed for approximately twenty minutes, and when I woke up I saw that both men had read the letter. It was a bit awkward talking to men on either side of me, but despite the circumstances I was able to ask each of them the four questions.

And each answered the fourth question, "Yes—I think I would!" What a thrill it was to present the message of God's love and forgiveness to them both— and to have each receive Christ with me as we prayed together.

OTHER HELPFUL QUESTIONS

Again, let me emphasize that without the proper motivation (love) these questions could sound like an inquisition. So it is vital that you ask them gently, with a friendly expression on your face and a caring tone in your voice.

Other questions which have proven effective in guiding a conversation toward Christ include:

•"In your opinion, what is the greatest spiritual need in the world today?"

•"Where do you see yourself on your spiritual journey?"

•"How would you like to know personally the God to whom you've prayed all your life?" (appropriate for someone with a religious background but who doesn't know Christ personally)

•"If you were to die today, do you know for sure you would go to heaven?"

If "yes": "On what basis do you know?"

If "no": "Would you like to be sure?"

Let me encourage you to memorize these questions. Practice asking them in a confident, natural way. Then, as the Lord leads, put them to work in your conversations to help lead others into a discussion of the gospel.

REMEMBER "LETUS"

Love others genuinely. *Establish* rapport. *Talk* about Jesus. *Use* stories if time allows. And utilize a *Sequence* of questions to lead in to the gospel presentation. In the next chapter, I'll show you how the particular gospel presentation I use was born, and why it is so effective today.

SUMMARY

●Friendship evangelism has its place, especially among close friends, office associates and family members.

●However, friendship evangelism can also be used as an easy excuse for failing to share the gospel. Therefore, it is important to also live by the principle of initiative evangelism.

●You can guide a conversation toward Jesus naturally by using the LETUS acrostic:

    L ove
    E stablish rapport
    T alk about Jesus
    U se stories (if time allows)
    S equence of questions

FOR REFLECTION AND ACTION

1. Have you allowed the philosophy of friendship evangelism to prevent you from sharing Christ when you've had opportunity?

2. Resolve today to make initiative evangelism your guiding principle in sharing your faith with others.

3. During the next week, set aside the time to write out your three-minute testimony. Then memorize it and practice giving it.

4. Memorize the suggested sequences of questions in this chapter. Practice them with a fellow believer.

*Sometimes we make the gospel message
so cumbersome that we fail to communicate
the essential truths of God's Word*

❧ 8 ❧

THE POWER OF SIMPLICITY

After my lecture to a group of pastors, one pastor lingered behind until I was through greeting the others. Finally, as the room was nearly empty, he approached me and introduced himself.

"I've been witnessing for years," he said, frustration tinging his voice. "But I've seen very few people receive Christ as a result of my efforts. Can you tell me what I'm doing wrong?"

"What do you say when you seek to introduce a person to Christ?" I asked.

He explained his presentation, which was long, complicated and sermonic. I sensed that the large number of Bible verses he used, and his lengthy commentary on each verse, confused most people and hindered them in making an intelligent decision.

"Let me encourage you to try an experiment," I challenged him. "Let me give you a gospel booklet that is concise, to-the-point, and focuses on Jesus Christ. Use it in all your witnessing opportunities for the next thirty days and then let me know what happens."

In only two weeks, he called me. The voice on the phone was ecstatic. "Bill, I can hardly believe it! By simply reading through the booklet with others, I've seen more people come to Christ in the last two weeks than I had previously seen in several months."

FAILURE TO COMMUNICATE

Sometimes we Christians don't like to admit it, but we often are guilty of making the gospel presentation so boring and cumbersome that we fail to communicate the essential truths of God's Word. There are so many Scriptures to choose from, and so many comments we can add to those Scriptures, that it's difficult to know what to include and what to leave for later.

In addition, many of us who have been believers for years may tend to think we're well beyond such simple truths as "For God so loved the world . . ." and as a result, we tend to over-intellectualize our presentation of the gospel.

My pastor friend, and thousands of others like him, have discovered one of the most dynamic principles of effective witnessing: *the power of simplicity.*

I am convinced that one of the reasons for the phenomenal effectiveness we see in the ministry of such men as Dwight L. Moody and Billy Graham is the simplicity of their message. Consistently, these men have focused on Jesus Christ through the use of just a few very fundamental truths. And their simple, consistent message has brought millions into God's kingdom.

A few years ago, one of our country's most renowned Christian scholars asked if he could share some of his concerns with me. He has always been a true friend, and I love and respect him dearly. But during this particular visit, he counseled, "Bill, you're the head of one of the most dynamic Christian movements in the world. But you come across as being too simple—almost anti-intellectual. You need to be more scholarly and impressive in your speaking and writing."

I considered his words for a moment, but knew what my answer would be. "Did it ever occur to you," I responded, "that Jesus Christ spoke so simply that even the illiterate masses responded gladly?"

His mouth literally dropped open. He appeared stunned, as though I had struck him. After a few moments' thought, he admitted, "You know, I have never thought of it that way . . . you're right. Sometimes we become so engrossed in our doctrine and language that we don't think about true communication."

As Vonette and I launched the ministry of Campus Crusade for Christ at UCLA in 1951, we learned very quickly that college students—whether they majored in phys. ed. or philosophy— weren't impressed with a complex, philosophical communication of the gospel.

What impressed them was Jesus Christ—who He is, what He did for them, and how they can know Him personally. So, during the first several years of the ministry, we gave a studied effort to making the gospel presentation as clear and simple as we possibly could.

God blessed the effort, and we saw students, student leaders, All-American athletes, fraternity and sorority officers, professors, and college officials come to Christ. Many of these new believers went on to full-time Christian work; others now proclaim Christ confidently in their chosen careers; and many joined our ministry and began to spread the work to other campuses across the country.

"PRESENTATION FATIGUE"

What I did not realize, however, was the need for consistency and uniformity in one's portrayal of the gospel. During summer staff training in 1956, one of our speakers was an outstanding Christian sales consultant. He emphasized that a successful salesman must develop a clear, simple, understandable presentation that he can use over and over again. Salesmen call this the "KISS" principle: *"Keep It Simple, Stupid."* But

then he warned that when a salesman grows tired of
hearing himself give the same message and develops
"presentation fatigue," he often changes the presentation and loses his effectiveness.

His next statement startled me. "Now in sharing
Christ, we need to develop a simple, understandable,
logical presentation just like the successful salesman
does," he told the audience. "And we need to stick with
that message and not yield to presentation fatigue."

I wasn't sure I agreed with him. It seemed that
God would honor spontaneity—sharing "as the Spirit
leads"—more than a prepared, "canned" approach. But
if his first statement startled me, the next remark almost knocked me from my chair.

"Your leader, Bill Bright, thinks he has a special
message for each of the different groups he speaks to.
He's ministered on Skid Row, in prisons, and now to
college students and lay people. Now I have never heard
him speak, but I would be willing to wager that he has
only one message for everyone. Basically, he tells them
all the same thing."

I squirmed in my seat and hoped that my resent-
ment of his comments didn't show in my face. How
could I, or anyone else truly committed to serving God,
not be led of the Spirit to speak with originality in
every situation? And how could this speaker have the
audacity to embarrass me like this in front of my staff?

When the meeting was over I was still feeling irritated over the speaker's message. But as I began to
reflect on exactly what I did say in various witnessing
opportunities, I asked myself: *Do I share the same basic
message with everyone? Is my message really* that *simple?*

GREAT PREACHER, OR GREAT SAVIOR?

Early in my Christian life, I had heard a brilliant
orator speak at Hollywood Presbyterian Church, and
he mesmerized the congregation with his eloquence.

Since I had studied speech and drama in high school and college, it seemed only logical that God had also chosen me to become an eloquent orator for the Lord. Before long, however, God sent a man to speak to us in seminary, and he challenged us with this thought: "When you come down from the pulpit, will people comment on what a great preacher you are, or on what a great Savior you serve?"

. That burst my bubble in a hurry. He was right, of course. I determined then that it was more important for people to comment that I served a great Savior than that I was a great preacher.

So after the salesman's talk at our summer staff training, I wrote down my basic presentation and was amazed to discover that he had been right. Without realizing it, I had been saying basically the same thing in every witnessing situation, whether to men in prison or on Skid Row, or to students, business leaders, or university professors. And my gospel presentation had proven effective in every setting.

THE FOUR SPIRITUAL LAWS

What I wrote that afternoon is now known as "God's Plan for Your Life," a positive, twenty-minute presentation which I asked the staff to memorize and use in their witnessing. Within one year, our combined effectiveness in sharing Christ was dramatically multiplied.

Eventually we felt the need for a shorter version, so I prepared an outline, complete with key Scripture verses and diagrams. Again, I had the staff memorize it, and for several years we would actually write it out on the back of the Van Dusen letter as we shared Christ with others. But as more and more lay people became involved in our training conferences, it became apparent that we needed to make the presentation available in printed form.

That's how the Four Spiritual Laws booklet was

born. It helps the reader to see how, just as there are physical laws which govern the physical universe, so there are spiritual laws (principles) which govern man's relationship with God. Key verses illustrate the validity of these principles, and simple diagrams help the reader apply the concepts to his own life.

We don't believe this portrayal of the gospel is the only way to present Christ, or that it's even the best way. But we can testify that many millions of people around the world have received Jesus Christ as Savior and Lord through this direct, simple presentation. Millions of Christians, including seminary professors and pastors, have discovered that this little booklet has dramatically helped their witness. Approximately 1 1/2 billion copies are in print in all major languages of the world, and at least fifty other Christian organizations have adapted the booklet for their own use.

In addition to the popular gold booklet titled "Have You Heard of the Four Spiritual Laws," we now also publish the Four Spiritual Laws with a bright green cover using the approach, "Would You Like To Know God Personally?" The message inside is basically the same, but now people can choose the approach which is most comfortable for them.

THE POWER OF SIMPLICITY

There is power in simplicity. For example, my friend Frank has a twenty-year-old cousin, a computer whiz who likes to think everything through in scientific terms. Frank's cousin mentioned to him one day that he wondered about the existence of God. "You know," Frank said, "I believe that just as you have physical laws that govern science, there are also spiritual laws that govern man's relationship with God. Here's a booklet that explains it."

Frank read aloud through the Four Spiritual Laws booklet, and it made sense to his cousin. The young man eagerly prayed the suggested prayer at the end to ask Jesus Christ into his life, then took the booklet and led his fiancée to Christ.

A few years ago I was visiting some dear friends, a doctor and his wife, and they asked if I would talk to her brother about Christ. "He's not a Christian but he's a wonderful person," they explained. He is a respected economist and one of America's foremost businessmen. "We'll set up an appointment for you," they assured me.

A few weeks later, when I met her brother, we chatted for a few minutes about world conditions and the urgency of the moment in which we live. "You know," I offered, "I think the only one who can help us face these crises is Jesus Christ."

I watched his face for response. "I sure agree with that," he nodded.

"I have something I want to show you." I pulled out a Four Spiritual Laws booklet, held it so he could read along, and read through the gospel presentation. After each principle, he offered, "That makes sense. I agree with that."

We read through the suggested prayer. "Does this prayer express the desire of your heart?" I asked.

"It sure does."

"Would you like to pray it right now?"

"I sure would."

So together we prayed asking the Lord to come into his life.

About six months later I visited him at his office in New York City. "You know, my life has made a 180-degree turn since I met you," he smiled.

A PASTOR'S FIRST EXPERIENCE

The stories go on and on. I think of a nationally known pastor who had been in the ministry for years. He attended a meeting where I spoke about walking in the Spirit, and he told me later that he now under-

stood and was able to personalize the ministry of the
Holy Spirit for the first time. About five months later
he called me, late at night, rejoicing that he had just
led his first person to Christ.

He is one of the most famous pastors in America,
and I'm sure that thousands have received the Lord
through his TV and church ministry. But he had never
personally led someone to Christ. His daughter had
taken our training, where she learned how to use the
Four Spiritual Laws booklet, and then passed her training on to him.

U.S. SENATOR RECEIVES CHRIST

U. S. Senator Bill Armstrong of Colorado recalled
in *Worldwide Challenge* magazine how the Four
Spiritual Laws booklet was a factor in his personal
decision to receive Christ:

> At the age of twenty-five I was elected to the State
> House of Representatives and then to the State Senate
> for eight years. In 1972 I was elected to the United
> States Congress. This kind of success was satisfying
> and challenging, but in spite of such accomplishments
> my life was shallow.
>
> After a few years in Washington, my wife Ellen
> began to seriously study the Bible, meeting with dedi-
> cated Christians who led her to a relationship with
> Jesus Christ. As she explained her new relationship to
> me, I realized that she had discovered something worth-
> while and meaningful that could also become meaning-
> ful for me. For the first time I understood that being a
> Christian is far more than merely belonging to a church
> or trying to live a good life.
>
> In November, 1975, through the encouragement of
> one of my colleagues, I heard Bill Bright speak. Later,
> Dr. Sam Peeples, one of Bill's associates from the Chris-
> tian Embassy in Washington, took me through the Four
> Spiritual Laws booklet, explaining how I could receive
> Christ. As we prayed together, I asked Jesus Christ to
> forgive my sins and to be my Savior and Lord. It was
> an easy decision to make because I knew that something

vital was missing in my life—something only Christ could provide.

My life began to change immediately, not in a single moment, but gradually each day. Most significantly, Christ became the center of our family life. I desired to be an example to my family of trusting the Lord with all of our day-to-day concerns.

My relationship with Christ has also given me a new perspective on Congress. As a senator, I pray each day that God will take control of my life so that my judgments and decisions will be made with His wisdom and discernment. Of course, I don't claim that the votes I cast are necessarily the Lord's votes, or that votes on the opposing side are against Him. But I strive to do what I think is right as I trust the Lord to lead me.

INCLUDES ALL THE ESSENTIAL TRUTHS

Occasionally, I have heard it said that the Four Spiritual Laws presentation is too simplistic—that anything this brief must omit some essential concepts. For many years, in our training conferences for students, lay people and pastors, we asked participants to help us list everything they felt a person should know before he could make an intelligent decision for Christ.

We usually received between twenty-five and fifty suggestions, all of which were listed on a chalkboard. The lists invariably included:

Man is sinful.

Man is lost.

God loved us so much that He gave His Son.

Christ died for our sins.

Christ rose from the dead.

He wants to come in to every life.

We must repent.

We must be born again.

We must receive Jesus Christ.

To all who receive Him, to them God gives the right to become His children.

After all suggestions were exhausted, we read

through the Four Spiritual Laws booklet together, looking for every point listed on the chalkboard that was covered in Law One. These points were then erased from the board. We continued reading through Laws Two, Three and Four, following the same procedure. At the end of the booklet, the chalkboard was always clean. All the essential concepts—the distilled essence of the gospel—are contained in the Four Spiritual Laws booklet.

THE SIMPLE TO CONFOUND THE WISE

One of our former staff members, an avid Bible student who has since gone on to become a popular Bible teacher and bestselling Christian author, learned the hard way about presentation fatigue and the power of simplicity. For several years, he used the Four Spiritual Laws booklet in his daily witnessing opportunities, with great results. But the more he studied the Bible, the more he began to embellish his delivery with further insights and other doctrinal issues gleaned from his study.

One day he came to visit with me. "Bill, I just don't understand it. I love the people I'm sharing with. I make sure there's no unconfessed sin in my life. I don't think I come on too strong. But I'm just not getting the positive responses to the gospel that I did before."

"Are you doing anything different than you used to?" I asked.

It was as if someone turned on a light bulb behind his eyes. He realized that, much like the salesman with presentation fatigue, he had changed his communication of the gospel and it was not as effective.

"Let me challenge you to try an experiment. Use only the Four Spiritual Laws booklet for the next thirty days. Don't embellish it with your own thoughts or other issues. Go straight through it, just as we trained you. Then let's get together and see what has happened."

He went back to the basics, as contained in Four Spiritual Laws booklet, and the results were dramatic. People again responded enthusiastically to the gospel.

The Bible tells us that "God uses the simple to confound the wise," and we have seen evidence of this over and over again. There is power in simplicity.

SUMMARY

●We often tend to over-intellectualize the gospel; as a result, our conveyance of the good news can be more confusing than clear.

●We enhance our effectiveness of communication by using a basic system that consistently covers all the essential truths of the gospel in a clear, simple way.

●Over the years, Christians from all walks of life have found the Four Spiritual Laws effective in helping introduce family members, friends, neighbors, co-workers, and casual encounters to Jesus Christ.

FOR REFLECTION AND ACTION

1. Has your delivery of the good news been boring and cumbersome? If you had only five minutes to convey the essential elements of the gospel to someone, could you do it in a clear, easy-to-understand way?

2. Ask God to give you a teachable spirit as you study the next chapter.

❧ 9 ❧

SHARING THE GOOD NEWS

I n the first chapter, I told you of several Christians who had felt inadequate in sharing Christ with others. After just a few hours of training in how to use the Four Spiritual Laws booklet, each of them was able to introduce someone to the Lord.

Jackie led one of her neighbors to Christ, and her husband Steve led his mother and Jackie's father to Him.

Al used the presentation in a prison to introduce an inmate to the Savior.

Burt reports seeing "consistent results as others respond to God's love through my witness."

Kathy led her neighbor, Sue, to Christ.

All of these people, and thousands of others like them, are continuing to take the initiative to share Christ in the power of the Holy Spirit, and leaving the results to God. And God is honoring their faithfulness.

Like these fellow believers, you are about to discover how easy it can be to utilize the Four Spiritual Laws (as found in both booklets, "Have You Heard of the Four Spiritual Laws?" and "Would You Like To Know God Personally?") in your witnessing opportunities. In this chapter, we will proceed page-by-page through the first booklet so you can see how it presents the Word of God and guides the non-believer toward a decision for Jesus Christ. The principles you learn in this chapter are appropriate for either booklet.

RECOGNIZING THE BENEFITS

Over the years, those who have used the Four Spiritual Laws presentation have realized several consistent benefits:

1. It enables you to be prepared for practically any witnessing situation.

2. It gives you confidence because you know what you are going to say and how you're going to say it.

3. It makes it possible for you to be brief.

4. It can be used to open the conversation. You can simply say, "Have you heard of the Four Spiritual Laws?"

5. It begins on a positive note: "God loves you."

6. It presents the claims of Christ clearly.

7. It includes an invitation to receive Christ.

8. It offers suggestions for growth.

9. It emphasizes the importance of the church.

10. It enables you to stay on the subject.

11. It gives you something tangible to leave with the person, either to reinforce the commitment he's made or to consider for a later decision.

PREPARING TO SHARE

Pray.

As we've already emphasized, prayer is an essential foundation to successful witnessing. As you begin each day, ask God to make you sensitive and obedient to His leading as you interact with friends, loved ones, neighbors, co-workers, and casual encounters. Ask Him to prepare the hearts of those to whom He might lead you, and to give you wisdom in sharing His love. In addition, pray silently as you begin to share the gospel, that God would communicate through you in such a way that the hearer can make an intelligent, heart-felt decision.

Be sure you are controlled by the Holy Spirit.

At the start of each day, be sure Christ is "on the throne" of your life. If the Holy Spirit is not in control of your life, your efforts will come from legalism rather than love. Then, as the Holy Spirit makes you aware of sin in your life, breathe spiritually. Exhale the impure (confess any unconfessed sin) and inhale the pure (surrender control of your life to Christ, and appropriate the control and power of the Holy Spirit).

Always keep a supply of booklets handy.

Always keep two or three Four Spiritual Laws booklets in your pocket, wallet or purse. As you've seen by the true stories in this book, you never know when the opportunity will present itself to use one, or several. Most Christian bookstores stock them; or, you can order them directly from Here's Life Publishers (see mailing address in appendix E).

Memorize the presentation.

This isn't a must, as long as you have a booklet to help you. But it's inevitable that opportunities will arise to share the gospel when a booklet isn't available, or when it would be awkward to use one (*e.g.,* when speaking before a group of three or more).

With just a little worthwhile effort, you can easily memorize the text and verses of the presentation (key verses which every Christian should know). Mark, a layman who decided to memorize the first twelve pages of the booklet, was glad he did. One day while he was having coffee with his boss, the conversation turned toward spiritual values. Mark didn't have any booklets with him, but because he had memorized the presenta-

tion he was able to write out the four principles on a
napkin, diagrams and all. And there, in the doughnut
shop, Mark's boss asked Jesus Christ into his life.

"LETUS."
Review the LETUS acrostic from chapter 7, "How
to Guide a Conversation Toward Jesus." Reach out in
Love. Take time to *Establish rapport. Talk about Jesus*
(keep the conversation focused on Him). *Use stories*
from your own experience (your three-minute testimony) if time allows. Utilize a *Sequence of questions*
to lead in to the booklet.

PRESENTING THE FOUR SPIRITUAL LAWS

*Be sensitive to the leading of the Holy Spirit and
to the individual's interest.*
The simplest way to explain the Four Spiritual
Laws is to read the booklet aloud. However, be careful
not to allow the presentation to become mechanical.
Remember, you are not *preaching to* or even *reading
to* the listener; you are *sharing with.* You are introducing the person to the Lord Jesus Christ, and the Four
Spiritual Laws are simply a communication tool. Continually pray for God's love to be expressed through you.

Hold the booklet so it can be seen clearly.
Use a pen or pencil to keep the listener's eye focused
on the text.

Stick to the presentation.
There is nothing magical about the Four Spiritual
Laws. But over the years, our staff and the students
and lay people we have trained have learned that it is
usually best to share the text just as it is written. This
helps to assure that the essential basics of the gospel
are presented and that they don't get lost in peripheral
discussion.

Defer most questions, graciously.

When questions arise that would change the subject, explain that most questions are answered as you go through the booklet. In most cases, once the listener has seen the full presentation, his questions will be answered. If you're not sure whether his question is answered in the booklet, you can say, "That's an excellent question. Let's talk about it after we've read through the booklet." You'll find that the questions usually fade in importance as the listener sees the full presentation in its context.

Be sensitive as you share.

If there seems to be no response, stop and ask, "Is this making sense?" If the listener is interested but has time constraints, give him the booklet and encourage him to read through it that night. If he says he's not interested at all, give him the booklet and say, "Perhaps there'll come a time when spiritual things *are* of special interest to you—why don't you take this with you so you can study it when that time comes?"

There are times, such as on a noisy airplane, when I simply hand the booklet to a person and ask him to read it and tell me what he thinks. After he has read it, I'll touch on the highlights, then read the fourth law and the suggested prayer word-for-word.

If you're sharing with a small group . . .

Give each person a booklet. Pray with those who are interested in receiving Christ. If only one is interested, talk with him privately after the others have disbursed.

Be confident!

Be assured that if you are walking in the Spirit, it is indeed God's will for you to share your faith with this person. You have a divine appointment. Remember: *Success in witnessing is simply taking the initiative to share Christ in the power of the Holy Spirit, and leaving the results to God.* If you obey, no matter what the results, you cannot fail!

Have You Heard of the
Four Spiritual Laws?

PAGE 1: INTRODUCING THE BOOKLET

As you pull a Four Spiritual Laws booklet from your pocket or purse, you may wish to use one of these statements which have proven effective in bridging from the conversation to the booklet:

1. "Have you heard of the Four Spiritual Laws? [Then, from page 2], Just as there are physical laws that govern . . ."

2. "Could I get your opinion of a special booklet? The contents of this booklet have changed my life. It's called the Four Spiritual Laws, and it shows that just as there are physical laws that govern . . ."

3. "You know, I came across a little booklet that clearly explains how we can have a personal relationship with God [or, which clearly explains whatever subject you were talking about]. It's called the Four Spiritual Laws, and it shows that just as there are physical laws that govern . . ."

4. If you think the person may be a Christian but you're not sure, you could say, "I've just recently found a way to express my faith that really makes sense, and I'd like to share it with you. Have you heard of the Four Spiritual Laws?"

1

Just as there are physical laws that govern the physical universe, so are there spiritual laws which govern your relationship with God.

LAW ONE

GOD **LOVES** YOU, AND OFFERS A WONDERFUL **PLAN** FOR YOUR LIFE.

(References contained in this booklet should be read in context from the Bible wherever possible.)

2

God's Love

"For God so loved the world, that He gave His only begotten Son, that whoever believes in Him should not perish, but have eternal life" (John 3:16).

God's Plan

(Christ speaking) "I came that they might have life, and might have it abundantly" (that it might be full and meaningful) (John 10:10).

Why is it that most people are
not experiencing the abundant life?
Because . . .   3

PAGES 2 & 3: A POSITIVE STARTING POINT

Take a pen or pencil, hold the booklet so the listener can follow along with you, and begin reading. Use inflection to put life into your voice. Read at a moderate pace—neither too fast nor too slow. (Don't read the parenthetical material at the bottom of page 2).

Pages 2 and 3 establish the important fact that God loves the listener, and offers a wonderful plan for his or her life. While many non-Christians might expect a condemnatory assault, this presentation begins with the warmth of God's love.

2 LAW TWO

MAN IS **SINFUL** AND **SEPARATED** FROM GOD. THEREFORE, HE CANNOT KNOW AND EXPERIENCE GOD'S LOVE AND PLAN FOR HIS LIFE.

Man Is Sinful

"For all have sinned and fall short of the glory of God" (Romans 3:23).

Man was created to have fellowship with God; but, because of his stubborn self-will, he chose to go his own independent way and fellowship with God was broken. This self-will, characterized by an attitude of active rebellion or passive indifference, is evidence of what the Bible calls sin.

4

Man Is Separated

"For the wages of sin is death" (spiritual separation from God) (Romans 6:23).

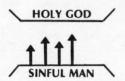

This diagram illustrates that God is holy and man is sinful. A great gulf separates the two. The arrows illustrate that man is continually trying to reach God and the abundant life through his own efforts, such as a good life, philosophy or religion.

The third law explains the only way to bridge this gulf . . .   5

PAGES 4 & 5: WHY MAN IS SEPARATED FROM GOD

Continue reading through pages 4 and 5, word for word. Glance at your listener occasionally as you read, both to help personalize what you're sharing and to gauge whether he's following along.

Pages 4 and 5 emphasize the reason people may not experience God's love and plan: sin. Romans 3:23 shows that sin is universal: *All* have sinned, and fall short of God's ideal. Romans 6:23 shows that the consequence of sin is death, or eternal separation from God. This is the toughest part for the listener to hear, but it is essential that he understand his separation from God.

You'll find the diagrams especially helpful in explaining the gospel. They give the listener a visual "hook" to grasp the truths of God's Word. Practice using them so that you can point to the diagram while explaining the related text.

3

LAW THREE

JESUS CHRIST IS GOD'S **ONLY** PROVISION FOR MAN'S SIN. THROUGH HIM YOU CAN KNOW AND EXPERIENCE GOD'S LOVE AND PLAN FOR YOUR LIFE.

He Died in Our Place

"But God demonstrates His own love toward us, in that while we were yet sinners, Christ died for us" (Romans 5:8).

He Rose from the Dead

"Christ died for our sins . . . He was buried . . . He was raised on the third day, according to the Scriptures . . . He appeared to Peter, then to the twelve. After that He appeared to more than five hundred . . ." (I Corinthians 15:3-6).

6

He Is the Only Way to God

"Jesus said to him, 'I am the way, and the truth, and the life; no one comes to the Father, but through Me' " (John 14:6).

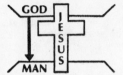

This diagram illustrates that God has bridged the gulf which separates us from Him by sending His Son, Jesus Christ, to die on the cross in our place to pay the penalty for our sins.

It is not enough just to know these three laws . . .   7

PAGES 6 & 7: THE MOST JOYFUL NEWS EVER ANNOUNCED

Here it is! God's provision for man's sin—how, through Jesus Christ, man can circumvent the kingdom of darkness and enter the kingdom of light. Pages 6 and 7 illustrate how Christ died for man's sin, rose from the dead, and is the only way to fellowship with God. God has bridged the gulf of separation through His Son, Jesus.

4

LAW FOUR
WE MUST INDIVIDUALLY **RECEIVE** JESUS CHRIST AS SAVIOR AND LORD; THEN WE CAN KNOW AND EXPERIENCE GOD'S LOVE AND PLAN FOR OUR LIVES.

We Must Receive Christ

"But as many as received Him, to them He gave the right to become children of God, even to those who believe in His name" (John 1:12).

We Receive Christ Through Faith

"For by grace you have been saved through faith; and that not of yourselves, it is the gift of God; not as a result of works, that no one should boast" (Ephesians 2:8,9).

When We Receive Christ, We Experience a New Birth.

(Read John 3:1-8.)

8

PAGES 8 & 9: PERSONALIZING THE GOOD NEWS

These pages emphasize the fact that it is not enough to merely give intellectual assent to the first three laws. One must personally *receive* Jesus Christ as Savior and Lord to know and live out God's love and plan. The listener is shown how to receive Christ, and what it involves.

Pay special attention to the two circles at the bottom of page 9. These are especially effective in helping the listener acknowledge where he stands with God. Recently I asked Lance, a skycap at an east coast airport, to read through the Four Spiritual Laws booklet while I gathered the luggage. When all the suitcases were accounted for, I asked him, "Which circle represents your life?"

"The one on the left," Lance replied.

"Which circle would you like to represent your life?"

"The one on the right," he said, resolutely.

Within just a few moments, Lance had discerned his standing with God, and realized that he wanted to receive Jesus Christ as his Lord and Savior. Together,

We Receive Christ by Personal Invitation

(Christ is speaking): "Behold, I stand at the door and knock; if any one hears My voice and opens the door, I will come in to him" (Revelation 3:20).

Receiving Christ involves turning to God from self (repentance) and trusting Christ to come into our lives to forgive our sins and to make us the kind of people He wants us to be. Just to agree intellectually that Jesus Christ is the Son of God and that He died on the cross for our sins is not enough. Nor is it enough to have an emotional experience. We receive Jesus Christ by faith, as an act of the will.

These two circles represent two kinds of lives:

SELF-DIRECTED LIFE
S — Self is on the throne
† — Christ is outside the life
● — Interests are directed by self, often resulting in discord and frustration

CHRIST-DIRECTED LIFE
† — Christ is in the life and on the throne
S — Self is yielding to Christ
● — Interests are directed by Christ, resulting in harmony with God's plan

Which circle best represents your life?
Which circle would you like to have represent your life?

The following explains how you can receive Christ: 9

we stood aside from the airport bustle and Lance prayed the suggested prayer. As we shook hands and as he wrote down his mailing address for me, he rejoiced at his new-found relationship with the Lord.

Learn the circle diagram well. It helps the listener visualize the real difference between the self-directed man and the Christ-directed man, and it encourages him to identify exactly where he stands. You'll find that it comes in handy in a variety of situations. Some people have even used the diagram successfully to *begin* a conversation about spiritual things.

YOU CAN RECEIVE CHRIST RIGHT NOW BY FAITH THROUGH PRAYER

(Prayer is talking with God)

God knows your heart and is not so concerned with your words as He is with the attitude of your heart. The following is a suggested prayer:

"Lord Jesus, I need You. Thank You for dying on the cross for my sins. I open the door of my life and receive You as my Savior and Lord. Thank You for forgiving my sins and giving me eternal life. Take control of the throne of my life. Make me the kind of person You want me to be."

Does this prayer express the desire of your heart?

10 If it does, pray this prayer right now, and Christ will come into your life, as He promised.

PAGE 10: A SUGGESTED PRAYER

One receives Christ not by prayer, but by faith. Prayer, however, is a tangible, conscious way of expressing faith and of "opening the door" of one's life to Christ. The suggested prayer on this page contains several important acknowledgments and commitments on the part of the listener, so read through it carefully with him.

Then come the two most important questions you will ask during the entire witnessing opportunity:

1. "John, does this prayer express the desire of your heart?"

2. "Would you like to pray this prayer, right now?"

Do not be shy at this point. This is where the listener needs your confident, calm leadership. When he says "yes," have him repeat the prayer after you, a phrase at a time. (We'll discuss in the next chapter what to do if the listener is hesitant or says "no.") When you have finished praying together, take a moment to congratulate him, then say, "Now let me ask you a few questions just so you understand what has just happened . . ." Proceed to page 11.

How to Know That Christ Is in Your Life

Did you receive Christ into your life? According to His promise in Revelation 3:20, where is Christ right now in relation to you? Christ said that He would come into your life. Would He mislead you? On what authority do you know that God has answered your prayer? (The trustworthiness of God Himself and His Word.)

The Bible Promises Eternal Life to All Who Receive Christ

"And the witness is this, that God has given us eternal life, and this life is in His Son. He who has the Son has the life; he who does not have the Son of God does not have the life. These things I have written to you who believe in the name of the Son of God, in order that you may know that you have eternal life" (I John 5:11-13).

Thank God often that Christ is in your life and that He will never leave you (Hebrews 13:5). You can know on the basis of His promise that Christ lives in you and that you have eternal life, from the very moment you invite Him in. He will not deceive you.

An important reminder . . .   11

PAGE 11: ASSURANCE OF SALVATION

Ask the questions at the top of page 11 to help the new believer comprehend the promises of God's Word. He can be assured that, because God and His Word are reliable, Christ is now in his life.

And, because God and His Word are reliable, he now has eternal life. Read through 1 John 5:11-13 to affirm this fact. You might ask at this point, "John, according to God's Word, when you die what is going to happen to you?" (He will have eternal life in heaven according to 1 John 5:11-13, John 3:16, Romans 6:23.)

DO NOT DEPEND UPON FEELINGS

The promise of God's Word, the Bible — not our feelings — is our authority. The Christian lives by faith (trust) in the trustworthiness of God Himself and His Word. This train diagram illustrates the relationship between **fact** (God and His Word), **faith** (our trust in God and His Word), and **feeling** (the result of our faith and obedience) (John 14:21).

The train will run with or without the caboose. However, it would be useless to attempt to pull the train by the caboose. In the same way, we, as Christians, do not depend on feelings or emotions, but we place our faith (trust) in the trustworthiness of God and the promises of His Word.

12

PAGE 12: "YOU MAY NOT *FEEL* DIFFERENT"

Page 12 addresses the question of feelings. Some people have dramatic conversions, while for others it's a calm, quiet decision. Continue reading through the text word for word, emphasizing how the train diagram illustrates the proper sequence. We have *faith* in the *fact* of God's Word. *Feelings* are a result of our faith, not a cause of our faith. Some days our feelings might be top-o-the-world, while on other days they may be so-so—but the *fact* of God's trustworthiness remains constant.

NOW THAT YOU HAVE RECEIVED CHRIST

The moment that you received Christ by faith, as an act of the will, many things happened, including the following:

1. Christ came into your life (Revelation 3:20 and Colossians 1:27).
2. Your sins were forgiven (Colossians 1:14).
3. You became a child of God (John 1:12).
4. You received eternal life (John 5:24).
5. You began the great adventure for which God created you (John 10:10; II Corinthians 5:17 and I Thessalonians 5:18).

Can you think of anything more wonderful that could happen to you than receiving Christ? Would you like to thank God in prayer right now for what He has done for you? By thanking God, you demonstrate your faith.   To enjoy your new life
                                                                    to the fullest . . . 13

PAGE 13: SUMMARY OF THE NEW LIFE

Page 13 is a quick overview of what transpired in the new believer's life when he received Christ. You'll want to encourage him to take the booklet home, open his Bible, and look up each of the references in context to affirm that God has indeed worked a miracle of love in his life. If time allows, have prayer together as suggested at the bottom of page 13, thanking God for what He has done.

SUGGESTIONS FOR CHRISTIAN GROWTH

Spiritual growth results from trusting Jesus Christ. "The righteous man shall live by faith" (Galatians 3:11). A life of faith will enable you to trust God increasingly with every detail of your life, and to practice the following:

G Go to God in prayer daily (John 15:7).

R Read God's Word daily (Acts 17:11)—begin with the Gospel of John.

O Obey God moment by moment (John 14:21).

W Witness for Christ by your life and words (Matthew 4:19; John 15:8).

T Trust God for every detail of your life (I Peter 5:7).

H Holy Spirit—allow Him to control and empower your daily life and witness (Galatians 5:16,17; Acts 1:8).

14

FELLOWSHIP IN A GOOD CHURCH

God's Word admonishes us not to forsake "the assembling of ourselves together. . ." (Hebrews 10:25). Several logs burn brightly together; but put one aside on the cold hearth and the fire goes out. So it is with your relationship to other Christians. If you do not belong to a church, do not wait to be invited. Take the initiative; call the pastor of a nearby church where Christ is honored and His Word is preached. Start this week, and make plans to attend regularly.

SPECIAL MATERIALS ARE AVAILABLE FOR CHRISTIAN GROWTH.

If you have come to know Christ personally through this presentation of the gospel, write for a free booklet especially written to assist you in your Christian growth.

A special Bible study series and an abundance of other helpful materials for Christian growth are also available. For additional information, please write Campus Crusade for Christ International, San Bernardino, CA 92414.

You will want to share this important discovery . . . 15

PAGES 14 & 15: GROWTH SUGGESTIONS

Here is a mini-course on what to do to grow in the new-found relationship with Jesus Christ. Encourage the new believer to study these on his own, too.

We strongly believe in, and are committed to serving, the local church. A new believer needs to find a fellowship of loving, committed Christians who love the Lord and His inspired Word, and who will encourage and strengthen his walk with God.

We'll talk further about follow-up in chapter 11, "How To Disciple the New Believer," but it's important to note here that there is a wide variety of helpful follow-up materials you can use with a new convert, either in person or by mail. Some of the most effective are listed in appendix E.

AFTER THE PRESENTATION

I cannot stress enough the importance of follow-up for the new believer. If you live in close proximity, always make an appointment to get together within forty-eight hours of his decision (preferably, within twenty-four hours). He will likely have questions and perhaps will be wrestling with a variety of emotions, and you can help him get a solid footing for his new walk with God.

If the new believer is a casual encounter, commit yourself to conscientious mail and phone follow-up. Try to phone him within twenty-four hours to assure him you are praying for him, to answer any questions he might have, and to encourage him to study and work through the material you will be sending him. Then, mail your first letter and follow-up piece within twenty-four hours of his decision.

More on this in chapter 11. In either case, it is essential that you:

1. Give the new believer your address and phone number.

2. Get his address and phone number.

3. Give him the copy of the Four Spiritual Laws booklet, and encourage him to read through it again that night. It is also important that he begin to study the New Testament, beginning with the Gospel of John. Encourage him to read the first three chapters that night before going to bed.

4. If you live in close proximity, set up a personal appointment to meet again within forty-eight hours; if you don't live nearby, ask permission to call to "see how it's going."

Note: If the new believer is of the opposite sex, I strongly recommend that you have a trusted friend of the same gender do the follow-up. I have often told women, for example, "I know a sharp Christian woman whose background is very similar to yours. Would you mind if I had her contact you?" This precaution can prevent potential misunderstandings and mixed-up emotions.

PULLING IT ALL TOGETHER

In our training conferences, we pair our conferees to practice delivery of the Four Spiritual Laws one-on-one. Let me encourage you to find a friend with whom you can practice, to shake out the initial jitters you might feel as you begin to read through the booklet aloud. Have your friend be a "friendly listener" at this point, posing no objections or questions. The aim is to get you comfortable with the basic presentation. In the next chapter, we'll look at how to handle some potential questions and smokescreens which might come your way.

SUMMARY

●There is a host of benefits to you in using a consistent presentation of the gospel such as the Four Spiritual Laws.

●Always keep two or three copies of the Four Spiritual Laws booklet with you.

●Follow the text closely. It has been proven effective in millions of situations. As you read, hold the booklet so the listener can follow along. Read with feeling.

●If you are short of time, try to at least get through page 12. If time does not allow for a full presentation, give the booklet to the listener and encourage him to read through it that night.

●Always try to get the new believer's name, address and phone number for follow-up.

FOR REFLECTION AND ACTION

1. Read aloud through the Four Spiritual Laws presentation at least three times, as if you were sharing it with someone.

2. Memorize the questions/comments on page 121 to help you bridge from conversation to the booklet. Practice them aloud so that they feel and sound natural to you.

3. Ask a positive Christian friend to pose as listener while you practice the bridges and the presentation.

4. Ask the Lord in prayer: "Lord, with whom do you want me to share this good news first?" Commit to Him that you'll be obedient to His leading when the first opportunity comes.

5. Obtain a quantity of Four Spiritual Laws booklets from your local Christian bookstore, or order directly from Here's Life Publishers (see mailing address in appendix E). Choose the title with which you are most comfortable: "Have You Heard of the Four Spiritual Laws?" or "Would You Like To Know God Personally?"

❧ 10 ❧

HOW TO HANDLE HOSTILITY, QUESTIONS AND RESISTANCE

"I don't believe in God, I don't believe in the Bible, and I don't believe in Christ and Christianity."

Ken's eyes flared at me from under the blond hair on his forehead as he cornered me after a campus lecture on the deity of Jesus Christ. He was a philosophy student, and I learned later from some other students that he seemed to delight in tearing Christianity apart. He seemed ready to tear *me* apart that night.

I put my hand on his shoulder and asked, "Why don't we sit down and talk?"

As we pulled two chairs into position for conversation, I quickly asked God for wisdom. He seemed to be reminding me: *Don't argue. Ask questions to find out why he feels the way he does.*

"Tell me what you don't believe about the Bible," I began.

"I just don't believe it. It's filled with all kinds of contradictions and myths." Ken slouched back in his chair, his arms folded tightly across his chest.

"Have you ever read it?"

"Oh, yes—I've read it through, cover to cover."

I handed Ken my Bible. "Can you show me what troubles you?"

"Well, there are thousands of contradictions . . ." his voice faded as he thumbed at the pages.

"Ken, if you'll show me just one problem or contradiction, maybe we can talk about it."

By now, Ken was flustered. He leaned forward, elbows on knees, and leafed through the Bible halfheartedly, realizing he couldn't produce evidence to back up his contentions.

"You say you've read the Bible, Ken?"

"Yes."

"How long ago did you read it?"

"Some time ago."

"How long? How old were you when you read it?"

"Oh . . . I guess I was twelve."

"Are you letting what you read when you were twelve years old influence your lifelong decisions? Ken, I think I understand how you're feeling. In my days of agnosticism, I would often parrot what I had heard other agnostics say, without checking the facts for myself. But do I discern, Ken, that the real reason you've come to me tonight is that you really want to know God personally?"

He leaned back in his chair and his cheeks bellowed as he exhaled loudly. "Yes," he sighed. "I do."

"Would you like to examine what Jesus Christ Himself said about how to know God? Here's a booklet that explains it . . ."

Together, we went through the Four Spiritual Laws booklet, and Ken invited Christ into his life. We talked for quite awhile about his new commitment, prayed together, then rose to leave.

"Mr. Bright—" Ken stopped us, his hand on my arm.

"Yes?"

His blue eyes had been transformed from hostility to peace. "Thank you. Thank you for not letting my big mouth prevent you from showing me the truth."

Despite Ken's loud protests and seeming hostility, God had made special plans for him that night. Frankly, I don't enjoy confrontations, but I have learned from many experiences that, like Ken, people who initially respond to the gospel with hostility are often the ones who are the most ready to receive Christ. Deep down, they are crying out for help—their visible belligerence is only a smokescreen to hide their hurt and hunger.

"OVER MY DEAD BODY!"

I recall an invitation from a group of Christian students at UCLA to speak in their fraternity. Their president, who was known as one of the campus's heaviest drinkers and loudest critics of Christianity, protested: "Over my dead body!"

"OK," joked several of his brothers, all hefty athletes. "Over your dead body."

He stayed alive, however, and was present during the fraternity meeting. After my talk I invited anyone who wanted to become a Christian to see me afterward. Almost all of the men gathered around me—and he was one of the first to ask for an appointment.

When we were alone, he confided, "Because I'm always the life of the party, drinking and putting on an act, most of my friends think I'm happy. But I'm probably the most miserable guy on this campus, and I need God."

To the utter amazement of his fraternity brothers, this young man received Christ two days later, turned his life around, and became one of the campus's most active students for the Lord.

"ANOTHER RELIGIOUS FANATIC"

A series of meetings at the University of Houston brought me face to face with another philosophy major, Benjamin, an older student renowned for his intellect and for his anti-God activism. Our campus director invited Benjamin to visit with me at a coffee shop after a long day of meetings, and Benjamin welcomed the opportunity to "debate another religious fanatic."

The three of us visited for more than an hour, but it seemed like a classic case of non-communication. Benjamin would give lengthy quotes from atheistic philosophers, and when he stopped for breath I would tell him that God loves him and offers a wonderful plan for his life. He would then state that God couldn't exist, and I would reply that I had felt pretty much the same way when I was an agnostic, but Jesus had changed my life.

I had been up and running since before dawn, so I was exhausted. It didn't seem like the conversation was going anywhere and I suggested we call it a night.

"Would you mind dropping me off at my dorm?" Benjamin asked us.

I got in the back seat, thinking I'd get a start on some much-needed sleep. But before we pulled out of the driveway, Benjamin turned around in the front passenger's seat and said, "Mr. Bright, everything you said tonight hit me in the heart. And I'd like to receive Christ right now."

Needless to say, sleep suddenly lost its importance.

Benjamin had given no indication that he was close to accepting the claims of Christ. There had been no positive response during our awkward conversation. I hadn't been what you'd call profound in my verbal witness. But the Holy Spirit had prepared Benjamin's heart, and had used me in spite of my weariness to penetrate his facade and communicate God's love.

THE UNDERLYING MEANING

As you share Christ with others faithfully, you will occasionally encounter hostility, questions, and resistance. Be sensitive to the leading of the Holy Spirit. There is a time to bring an end to a conversation, give the listener something to read, and encourage him to invite Christ into his life when ready.

But you will also find that, in the majority of cases, a listener's initial resistance really signifies that he wants to know more . . . that his questions indicate he's sincerely interested in clarifying some important points . . . and that any initial hostility is in reality a mask to hide a deep-down cry for help.

GENERAL GUIDELINES

The purpose of this chapter is to help you guide the listener through such smokescreens so he can focus on the person of Jesus Christ and make an intelligent decision. Before we address specific objections which you might encounter, let's establish some important general guidelines:

1. *Never argue.*

Remember, your mission is to proclaim the good news, not to win an argument. Let the genuine *agape* love of God pervade your words, your tone of voice, and your facial expressions. Answer questions and ask questions, but do not argue.

2. *Don't try to reason within the listener's sphere of expertise.*

I studied philosophy, but I would have dug quite a hole for myself if I had tried to reason philosophically with Ken or Benjamin. I studied science, but I wouldn't fare well if I tried to reason from science with a scientist. So I try to stay focused on the person of Jesus Christ— His love, His death and resurrection, His gift of eternal life.

3. *Remember what God has commissioned you to do.*

Your task is to proclaim; it is God's task to convert. Share the claims of Christ thoroughly. Answer questions calmly, to the best of your ability. Give the listener ample opportunity to respond. In most cases, he will respond favorably. But if he doesn't, you have planted a seed—and you can trust God with the results.

Remember: *Successful witnessing is simply taking the initiative to share Christ in the power of the Holy Spirit, and leaving the results to God.*

4. *Try to get the listener into the Four Spiritual Laws as quickly as possible.*

Whenever appropriate, use the question or objection as a means to transition into the presentation. Many questions and objections will be resolved in the listener's mind as he sees the full context of the gospel.

5. *Appeal to the listener's intellectual integrity.*

No one wants to be "intellectually dishonest," but this is precisely the error which many people make when resisting God's Word: It is the one thing which they refuse to investigate objectively. By appealing to their intellectual integrity, you can help them see that they should indeed give the gospel a fair hearing.

6. *Always, if the listener rejects the gospel, leave him with something to read.*

Give him the Four Spiritual Laws booklet or a Gospel of John, along with a challenge to do the "30-Day Experiment." More on the "experiment" later; the principle is, literature distribution is the next-best thing to being there. So always give the listener something to take home for further study.

WHEN QUESTIONS MIGHT COME

Questions, resistance and objections may occur in one of three places during your sharing opportunity:

1. During lead-in conversation, prior to presentation of the Four Spiritual Laws;

2. During the presentation, particularly regarding the circle diagram on page 9;

3. Following the reading of the suggested prayer on page 10.

If an objection comes up during lead-in conversation, you can deal with it briefly and then actually use it to bridge into the Four Laws presentation. For example, your listener states, "I don't feel that God could love me after the things I've done." You could say, "You know, it's amazing—I've discovered that God loves us in spite of what we've done. In fact, I've come across a little booklet that explains it beautifully—would you like to see what the Bible says about God's love?"

If an objection comes up while you're reading through the booklet, remember to defer the question, graciously, to the end of the presentation. The only exception to this guideline is if the listener is obviously irritated and doesn't want you to continue. If this should happen, apologize: "I'm sorry if I have offended you. Here, why don't you keep the booklet and read through it yourself, when you're ready?"

If questions or objections are raised after you've invited the listener to pray the suggested prayer, *now* is the time to patiently address each question. You have laid the foundation by showing the four biblical principles. If his questions weren't answered by the context of the presentation, try to answer them now. Never push or rush a decision for Christ. When you sense that the listener's questions have been answered, you can gently ask, "Is there anything now that would prevent you from receiving Christ? How about doing it right now?"

THE 30-DAY EXPERIMENT

The person who contends "I don't believe" is usually more of a candidate for the kingdom than one who says, "I don't care." I have found that in many cases, those who say they don't believe in God, the Bible, or the deity of Christ are really people who have been hurt and have emotional scars. Perhaps they have been offended by an overly strict parent, an immoral Christian leader, or another adult who talked the Christian life but didn't live it. If this is not the case, it's possible that they are on some sort of prideful, intellectual kick.

Whether they profess atheism, agnosticism, militant humanism or honest doubt, an appeal to their intellectual integrity through the "30-Day Experiment" can bring dramatic results.

How does the "experiment" work?

A Christian student was dating a man who was rigorously antagonistic toward God. She asked me if I would talk with him, and when I arrived, he was absolutely furious.

"I don't care about your God," he fumed, "and I really don't care to talk to you." He made a few other choice comments, no expletives deleted.

I felt awkward, caught in the middle. Apparently, she had not told him or even asked him about my visit.

"Look, I'm sorry," I apologized. "I don't normally become involved in the middle of something like this. But before I go, I want to say this: You are dating a wonderful young Christian woman. You can ruin her life, and you have no right to have anything more to do with her, unless you let God take hold of your life."

He wouldn't even talk to me. His face was so red with anger that I can still feel the heat he generated. I moved to the edge of my chair to get up. "I want to leave you with this thought: You say you don't believe in God or the Bible. I'm going to ask you to perform an experiment, as a matter of intellectual integrity.

"Read the Bible every day, starting with the Gospel of John. One hour a day, for thirty days. And every day begin your reading with a prayer: *God, if You exist, and if Jesus Christ is your revelation to man and He truly died for my sins, I want to know You personally.*

"If you pray that prayer every day, and read the Bible for an hour objectively—as an honest seeker of truth—I think you'll know what I'm talking about."

He did not respond to my suggestion. As I left him

and his Christian girlfriend, I felt burdened that he would refuse to have anything to do with Christ and would ultimately ruin her life.

About four months later, his girlfriend received a letter from him. He had been traveling in Europe, and had begun to read the Bible. God had spoken to him through His Word, and he wrote his girlfriend:

I'm ecstatic! I performed the 30-Day Experiment your friend told me about, and I now know why you're so excited about Christ. I, too, have received Him as my Savior and Lord!

"WOULD YOU PERFORM AN EXPERIMENT?"

A young man present at an evangelistic breakfast at the University of Colorado told me that "this God business is a lot of nonsense." Of course, I had learned that often when people like him come to me, they're really hungry for God and (subconsciously) they're hoping I'll see through their facade and help them.

"Are you an honest person?" I asked.

"Of course I am."

"Would you perform an experiment?"

"Like what?"

"A scientist goes into the laboratory to do research without preconceived ideas. He goes with an open mind and considers all truth objectively. Would you be willing to perform an experiment for thirty days, as a matter of intellectual integrity?"

I described the 30-Day Experiment. "Well, I could do that," he shrugged.

"What are you doing today?" I probed.

"It happens to be my free day—that's why I'm here."

"I know you'll want to be intellectually honest about this, just like the objective scientist. Why don't you take the whole day and go read the Gospel of John. Read it and pray that if Jesus Christ is God, and He died for your sins, He will come into your life and be your Savior and Lord."

That evening I was speaking to a group of several hundred students. As I began, I looked out over the crowd. There, right in the middle of the auditorium, was this young man—beaming at me with a countenance that could have lighted the whole auditorium.

I could hardly wait until the meeting was over, and when I finished he darted through the crowd to meet me. "I did it," he grinned. "I did what you told me. I read the first, second, third, fourth chapters of John."

I'll never forget his next statement: "I was in the eighth chapter when Jesus stepped out of the pages of the Bible into my heart."

Let me encourage you to learn to appeal to one's intellectual integrity through the use of the 30-Day Experiment. You can use this approach in almost any situation where hostility, unbelief or doubt is expressed. The principle: *When in doubt about what to say, let God's Word do the talking.*

OTHER QUESTIONS AND SMOKESCREENS

Let's take a quick tour of other objections that may arise during a witnessing opportunity and suggested responses to them.

"I'm an atheist. There is no God."

"John, do you know everything there is to know?"

"Of course not. Even Einstein only scratched the surface of knowledge."

"Of all the knowledge in the world, what percent do you think you know? Eighty percent?"

"Oh, no! I'd do well to understand 1 or 2 percent."

"All right. But let's assume that you knew 80 percent. Isn't it at all possible that God could exist in that 20 percent of all knowledge you don't know?" (Bridge to Four Spiritual Laws.)

"I believe God is in all men."

"Nancy, do you think Jesus Christ was a liar?"

"Oh, no. He was probably the most moral person who ever lived."

"If He wasn't a liar, was He a deluded lunatic?"

"No—why do you ask that?"

"Well, there are only three choices. If He wasn't a liar, and if He wasn't a lunatic, then what He said had to be truth. As a matter of intellectual integrity, wouldn't you want to consider what He taught about man's relationship to God?" (Bridge to Four Spiritual Laws.)

"Jesus was a great teacher, and a moral person. But I don't believe He was God."

Use the Liar/Lunatic approach illustrated above. Then, when explaining the three choices, say, "If He wasn't a liar, and if He wasn't a lunatic, then what He said about Himself had to be truth. He had to be who He said He was. As a matter of intellectual integrity, wouldn't you want to consider what He taught about His relationship to God?" (Bridge to Four Spiritual Laws.)

"I think if we're good people and don't hurt anyone, we'll go to heaven."

Again, utilize the Liar/Lunatic approach. When explaining the third choice, say, ". . . then what He taught had to be truth. As a matter of intellectual integrity, wouldn't you want to consider what He taught about eternal life?" (Bridge to Four Spiritual Laws, and place special emphasis on Ephesians 2:8,9: "For by grace you have been saved through faith; and that not of yourselves, it is the gift of God; not as a result of works, that no one should boast.")

"I don't believe the Bible."

"Let me ask you a question. The main message of the Bible, which is unquestionably the most important literary work in history, is how a person may have eternal life. Do you understand what the Bible teaches about this?"

"I don't believe in eternal life."

"I'm not asking you what you believe, but what you understand. Don't you agree that it would be intellectually dishonest to reject the world's most important book without understanding even its main message?"

Most people at this point will guess that the way to have eternal life is through keeping the Ten Commandments or the Golden Rule, and by being honest and doing good things.

"John, that's an interesting answer, but it's opposite of what the Bible teaches. Now I know you want to be objective and exercise intellectual integrity. Don't you think the more intellectual approach would be to investigate what the Scriptures teach on this matter? Then you can make an intelligent decision whether to accept or reject it." (Bridge to Four Spiritual Laws.)

"I've seen too many hypocrites."

"Nancy, any time we look at men instead of at God we'll see sin and weaknesses. Christians are still human, and they'll still fail because God gives them freedom to choose whether He's in control or they are in control of their lives.

"Someone said, 'The church is a hospital for sinners, not a hotel for saints.' I also like the saying, 'The church is not a retail store, it's a repair shop.' That's so true—becoming a Christian doesn't mean we're perfect, just forgiven. We'll still sin, but as we allow God to control us, sin will become less and less appealing.

"But the important question is not 'What about the hypocrites?' Rather, it is 'What about *my* sin, and God's provision for it?' Would you like to investigate what Jesus Christ said about God's relationship to you?" (Bridge to Four Spiritual Laws.)

"I go to church, serve on such-and-such a committee,

and was raised in a good home."

"I realize that you have done all these things. But have you ever personally received Jesus Christ as Savior and Lord?"

"I'm not sure."

"Would you like to be sure?" (Transition to the Four Spiritual Laws.)

"I'm not interested."

"I understand. It's probably something you haven't had much opportunity to think about. But if you're like most people, it's possible that there will come a time in the future when spiritual matters *do* become important to you. I'd like to give you something that has meant a lot to me in this regard. Why don't you take it home and read it, and see what you think?" (Write your name, address and phone number on the back of the booklet and give it to him. Challenge him to undertake the 30-Day Experiment.)

Responses to the question, "Which circle best represents your life?" (page 9 of the Four Spiritual Laws booklet)

1. If the listener responds, "The circle on the left," simply continue through the presentation by asking the next question.

2. If he says, "I'm not sure," or "I'm in-between," or if he remains silent, simply continue through the booklet by asking the next question.

3. If the listener responds, "The circle on the right," continue through the booklet to show him how he can share his faith with others. You could say, "That's good—I'm delighted to hear that Christ is in your life. Let's finish reading the booklet so that you can use it to share your faith in Christ with someone else."

●If he is a Christian, the rest of the presentation will help him learn how to present the claims of Christ to others.

●If he is not a Christian, he may realize it after going through the suggested prayer.

●After reading the suggested prayer, ask, "Have you ever received Christ in the way this prayer expresses?" If he has, encourage him to use this presentation to witness to others. If he has not, give him the opportunity to invite Christ into his life right then, "to be sure without a doubt that you have received Christ into your life."

Responses to the question, "Which circle would you like to have represent your life?" (page 9)

1. If the listener answers, "The circle on the right," simply continue reading through the booklet with the transition at the bottom of the page: "The following explains how you can receive Christ."

2. If he answers that he's not sure, or if he remains silent, continue reading through the booklet.

3. If he responds, "The circle on the left," don't let it rattle you. Stay positive and loving. You could say, "John, at some time in your life you may want to receive Christ. So let me show you how you can invite Christ into your life so you'll know, when that time comes. Would that be all right?" Continue reading through the prayer.

Responses to the question, "Does this prayer express the desire of your heart?" (page 10)

1. If he says "yes," say, "Would you like to repeat the prayer after me as I read it a sentence at a time?" If he feels uncomfortable about praying aloud, you could ask him to read through the prayer silently, praying in his heart.

Be sensitive to his comfort level at this point. In many cases, if a person shows hesitancy to pray along with me, I'll give him the booklet and encourage him to pray the prayer silently. Or, if he does not wish to do so, I encourage him to pray this prayer when he gets home. On many occasions, such people have contacted me by phone or letter to let me know that they have done so.

2. If he says he would like to pray the prayer at home, say, "That would be fine. Many people like to do so in privacy. Let's just take a moment to preview what will happen in your life when you receive Christ tonight." Read the bottom section of page 11 and the five points on page 13.

3. If he says "no," maintain a positive and loving spirit. Again, you could say, "It's an important decision, and I'm glad you're not taking it lightly. Let me show you what would happen if you asked Christ to come into your life." Read the bottom section of page 11 and the five points on page 13.

"I'm not ready."

"It is an important decision—the most important one you'll make in your entire life because it affects how you'll spend eternity. So I appreciate the fact that you're not taking it lightly. But there may come a time when you are ready—would you take this booklet and read it so that, when the time comes, you'll know how to receive Christ?"

PLANTING THE SEED

Never let objections intimidate you. Handle them in the best way you can, and guide the conversation back to the suggested prayer. If the response is still negative, put your name, address and phone number on the back of the booklet and leave it with the listener. You'll find that quite often, the hesitant listener will re-read the booklet and receive Christ in the privacy of his home.

Challenge him to do the 30-Day Experiment. Then pray for him, leaving the results to God. You have planted a seed for God to nurture in His perfect timing.

When Chuck was a senior journalism major at the University of Missouri, he shared Christ with Dave, a promising freshman journalism student. Dave considered the gospel message carefully but responded, "I'm not ready for this kind of thing."

Well, I've planted a seed, Chuck thought, as he prayed for Dave. During the next year, he dropped by Dave's room often to discuss journalism and sports, but when Chuck graduated, Dave was still not a Christian.

In Dave's sophomore year he attended a campus lecture by Josh McDowell, who again emphasized the need for a personal relationship with Jesus Christ. By this time, Dave was ready—he invited Christ into his life and later began studying the Bible with a group of Christian students.

God moves in mysterious ways. Dave graduated with his journalism degree and joined the staff of Campus Crusade for Christ, where he now serves as editor of *Worldwide Challenge* magazine. One of his right-hand associate editors is Chuck, the young man who "planted the seed" years ago. Together, they impact thousands of lives for Christ as the magazine is sent to more than 100,000 homes every other month.

So never let hostility, questions and objections discourage you. God is sovereign—He has given you the duty and the privilege of sharing the gospel faithfully, intelligently, and lovingly—and you can leave the results to Him. Your task is simply to obey; His is to change the hearts of the men and women with whom you share.

SUMMARY

●In many cases, expressions of hostility simply mask an inner desire for God.

●By answering questions and objections calmly and with love, you can guide the listener through the smokescreens so he can make an intelligent decision.

●Never argue or attempt to cajole someone into a decision.

●Appeal to the listener's intellectual integrity

through the 30-Day Experiment.

●Utilize the Liar/Lunatic approach whenever he questions the existence of God, the deity of Christ, the reality of eternal life, or the need to receive Christ personally.

●Always, if a person rejects Christ, leave him with something to read.

FOR REFLECTION AND ACTION

1. Do not allow the possibility of tough questions, objections, or rejection to deter you from sharing the gospel. In most cases, none of these situations will even arise.

2. Memorize the basic concepts of the 30-Day Experiment and the Liar/Lunatic approach. You'll find that these two approaches alone can help you in almost every situation.

3. With your Christian friend, rehearse answers to the various responses to the circle questions (page 9, The Four Spiritual Laws) and to the invitation to pray (page 10).

4. Study the suggested responses to the other possible objections discussed in this chapter.

5. The Bible clearly states that God's Word will never return void (Isaiah 55:11). Ask yourself: *What does this biblical promise mean to me as I witness for Christ?*

Prompt, loving follow-up
will help the new Christian get a solid start
in his new life

❧ 11 ❧

HOW TO DISCIPLE THE NEW BELIEVER

Several years ago, one of our staff members handed me a copy of *Sports Illustrated*. The picture on the cover was of the recent Heisman Trophy winner, the year's best collegiate football player.

"Meet your great-grandson," the staff member said, grinning ear to ear.

"What do you mean?" I asked.

"Well," he explained, "you led Jim to Christ, Jim led me to Christ, and I led Steve [the Heisman Trophy winner] to Christ."

What a blessing it was for me to see how one young man, whom I'd had the privilege of introducing to Jesus Christ, was already directly responsible for two generations of new believers. He had taken the training I had shared with him, then passed it along to another who in turn was discipling still another.

The discipleship process is especially important for new Christians. During the days, weeks and months following their decision to receive Christ, they will encounter doubts, conflicting emotions, and questions about what they have done. They will continue to be exposed to that same negative, humanistic world that formed their B.C. (Before Christ) world view. Temptations will continue to hammer at them, often more intensively than before. And the people they love most may discount—even ridicule—their decision.

That's why follow-up is so vital to the new believer. He is just a babe in Christ, down from the mountaintop experience of new birth, thrust back into his hostile environment. He needs help in understanding God's love and provision for him and how living for Christ affects his daily walk.

When a mature Christian considers the value of a soul, which Jesus taught is worth more than all the wealth of the world, he will be eager to help each new Christian grow and become a true disciple.

DISCIPLING MODELED BY CHRIST, PAUL

Our Lord could have spent all His time in evangelism. But He spent much time discipling those closest to Him, especially the twelve. He considered discipling so important that He included it in His command to fulfill the Great Commission: ". . . Teach these new disciples to obey all the commands I have given you" (Matthew 28:20, TLB).

The apostle Paul took seriously our Lord's command. To the Colossians he wrote, "So everywhere we go we talk about Christ to all who will listen, warning them and teaching them as well as we know how. We want to be able to present each one to God, perfect because of what Christ has done for each of them" (Colossians 1:28, TLB).

In his second letter to Timothy, Paul counseled, "For you must teach others those things you and many others have heard me speak about. Teach these great truths to trustworthy men who will, in turn, pass them on to others" (2 Timothy 2:2, TLB).

THE MULTIPLICATION PRINCIPLE

While Jesus placed strong emphasis on witnessing, and the apostle Paul was influenced by His example and instructions, they did not stop there. They emphasized the importance of bringing new converts to spiritual maturity so they (1) would be strong in the Lord, and (2) would teach the things they had learned to others. Evangelism, discipleship and spiritual multiplication were intertwined in everything the Lord Jesus and the apostle Paul did, and this is why the early church grew so dramatically.

The same principle holds true today. In the early years of my personal ministry, I spent considerable time contemplating whether I should concentrate solely on evangelism, or pursue the dual objectives of evangelism and discipleship. After much thought and prayer, I decided that the Lord had called me to do both. So I worked intensively with those who became Christians through my ministry, to build them in their faith and to instruct them to reach and teach others. As others joined the staff, we continued to place a strong emphasis on both discipleship and evangelism.

Looking back, I'm glad I made that decision, for simple mathematics shows the wisdom of our Lord's emphasis on disciple-building. If you were to personally lead one person to Jesus Christ every day, and none of them introduced anyone else to the Lord, the result after thirty-five years would be almost 13,000 souls for Christ. However, if you were to teach those new believers how to introduce others to Christ, and they in turn taught *their* disciples how to witness, the thirty-five-year result would be in the multi-millions.

Obviously, life doesn't happen quite so neatly. It often is not possible to personally disciple everyone you've introduced to Christ. And, as in the Parable of the Sower, some people fall away; others are lukewarm and simply don't obey our Lord's imperative to share the gospel.

But the multiplication principle does illustrate how the world can indeed be changed through the lives of those who become true disciples. This is the goal we have sought to keep before us in the ministry of Campus Crusade for Christ, and I believe that it has been one of the keys to our growth and spiritual blessing.

"FOLLOW-UP": THE INITIAL STAGE

"Follow-up" is a term coined to describe the vital, initial stages of discipleship. Ideally, follow-up begins within twenty-four hours after the new believer's decision for Christ, and is done personally by either the person who led him to the Lord or a trusted Christian delegated to take on the task.

The discipler's job during follow-up is to provide encouragement, answer questions, and lend prayer support; to help the new believer understand and further commit himself to the lordship of Jesus Christ; to network the new convert with other Christians and a Bible-teaching church fellowship; and to help wean this "babe in Christ" from milk to solid food through a systematic beginning Bible study and a regular witnessing program.

WHEN THE DECISION IS MADE

You will recall that whenever someone receives Christ with you, it is important to get his address and phone number. If you live in close proximity, set an appointment to get together the next day (within two days at the most). Explain that you want to give him more information that will help him begin his new life. Encourage him to take the Four Spiritual Laws booklet home and re-read it that night to affirm God's love for him and the decision he has made. In addition, he should read the first three chapters of the Gospel of John that same night. Ask him to come to the first appointment with any questions he might have.

If you don't live close by, ask for permission to call him to see how he's getting along, then call the next day. Within that same twenty-four hour period, put a letter of encouragement in the mail, along with a copy of *How to Be Sure You Are a Christian,* the first of nine "Transferable Concepts" which are written to help the new Christian take his first steps in the faith. (The Transferable Concepts, and other recommended materials for witnessing and follow-up, are generally available at your local Christian bookstore. See appendix E for further information.)

THE FIRST MEETING

The first meeting (or first phone call) is a time to reinforce the significance of what God is now doing in the life of the new Christian. Here is what should be covered:

1. Questions the new believer may have.

2. The matter of feelings. Review the train diagram on page 12 of the Four Spiritual Laws booklet.

3. Assurance of salvation. *Ask:* "Where is Christ right now in relation to you?" Review Revelation 3:20. *Ask:* "If you were to die tonight, do you know without a doubt that you would go to heaven?" Review 1 John 5:11-13. *Ask:* "Will Jesus Christ ever leave you?" Review Hebrews 13:5.

4. Walk through the five facts on page 13, looking up and reading together the Scriptures that support each point:

●Christ has come into your life (Revelation 3:20; Colossians 1:27).

●Your sins have been forgiven (Colossians 1:14).

●You have become a child of God (John 1:12).

●You have received eternal life (John 5:24).

●You have begun the great adventure for which God created you (John 10:10; 2 Corinthians 5:17; 1 Thessalonians 5:18).

5. Give him a copy of the Transferable Concept,

How to Be Sure You Are a Christian. Ask him to read through it during the next two days, and set an appointment for another meeting (or phone call) within the next seventy-two hours. You could say, "John, it's really important that you get started properly in your walk with God. Would it be all right if we meet regularly to study the Bible together and see how it applies to our lives?"

6. Encourage him to begin reading the Gospel of John early in the morning, or at night before going to sleep. Introduce it as a historical account of the life of Jesus Christ and what His life means to us.

7. Pray together, thanking God for the salvation and new life He has brought to your friend.

THE SECOND MEETING

Whenever possible, your second follow-up meeting should be within three days of the first. This frequency at the beginning of the discipling process will help build a sense of positive momentum in the new Christian's growth pattern, and will help prevent doubts, questions and daily problems from overwhelming him.

1. Pray together, asking God to bless your time of fellowship.

2. Ask him if he has read *How to Be Sure You Are a Christian.* Answer any questions he has, then go through the questions in the booklet and help him phrase his answers to write in the spaces provided.

3. Find out how he's doing in reading the Gospel of John. You might ask, "What are the most meaningful truths you have discovered in your reading?" Do your best to answer questions (if you don't know an answer, be honest and say so; promise to get an answer to him as soon as possible). Encourage him to keep reading.

4. Give him the second Transferable Concept, *How to Experience God's Love and Forgiveness.* Ask him to read it through and answer the questions himself before the next meeting.

5. Invite him to church with you next Sunday. Offer a ride, and either take him to lunch or invite him home for lunch afterward.

(If you're doing follow-up over long distance, mail your new believer the recommended Transferable Concepts and discuss them briefly by phone. Encourage him to write you with further questions and regular reports on how he's doing spiritually. Through your pastor or other reliable contacts, locate a good church in your new friend's locale and encourage him to attend. Drop the pastor of that church a note encouraging him to invite your friend to the next Sunday's activities.)

6. Pray together, and set up your next appointment for approximately one week from today.

SUBSEQUENT MEETINGS

There are nine Transferable Concepts, and we have found the series to be extremely effective in helping the new believer. Your next several meetings could cover some or all of the remaining concepts:

- *How to Be Filled with the Spirit*
- *How to Walk in the Spirit*
- *How to Love by Faith*
- *How to Pray*
- *How to Witness in the Spirit*
- *How to Introduce Others to Christ*
- *How to Help Fulfill the Great Commission*

Always plan and prepare, but never let follow-up meetings be so rigid that you fail to deal with questions and concerns your disciple might have. Your main objective is to help him develop a lifestyle of love, faith, obedience and witnessing.

LEAD BY EXAMPLE

Let your personal enthusiasm for God and His Word be evident in your daily walk. We cannot expect others to become students of the Word unless we are students of the Word. We cannot expect them to lead others to Christ unless they see us leading others to Christ. By example, you can role-model practical Christian living: victory over circumstances, faith in troubled times, a godly, moral, Christ-centered lifestyle; and love, joy, peace, patience, kindness, goodness, faithfulness, gentleness and self-control.

Obviously, however, you cannot afford to wait for inner perfection before you disciple another person. Be candid with him about your own weaknesses and struggles. Let him see you "breathe spiritually" when you fail; invite him to pray with you through tough times. You will find that, in addition to teaching by example, you will actually grow *with* your disciple.

PRAY FOR HIM

The Lord Jesus prayed for His disciples and for all who would ultimately believe, including us (John 17). The apostle Paul also prayed for all whom the Lord had placed in his charge. For example, in Ephesians 1:17,18 (TLB) he wrote, "I pray for you constantly, asking God, the glorious Father of our Lord Jesus Christ, to give you wisdom to see clearly and really understand who Christ is and all that He has done for you. I pray that your hearts will be flooded with light so that you can see something of the future He has called you to share."

Pray daily for the new believer.

TEACH SPIRITUAL GROWTH

As you continue to meet with your new Christian friend, follow-up will mature into discipleship as you take him from "milk" to "solid food." Teaching the truths necessary for Christian growth involves a number of important aspects:

Be sure that he has assurance of his salvation. Revelation 3:20, Hebrews 13:5 and 1 John 5:11-13 are essential promises which every new Christian should memorize. Review these passages with him several times during the first few weeks, repeating the questions: (1) "Where is Jesus Christ right now in relation to you? How do you know?" (Revelation 3:20 and Hebrews 13:5); (2) "When you die, what will happen to you?" (1 John 5:11-13).

Encourage him to make Christ the Lord of his life, according to Romans 12:1,2; Galatians 2:20; and similar passages. Man is so created that we do not find fulfillment until we have acknowledged our accountability to God and have obeyed His commands. Emphasize that there are no joyful, fulfilled, *disobedient* Christians. Conversely, there are no truly *obedient* Christians who do not experience joy regardless of circumstances.

Teach him by being an example, by instructing him in God's Word and by introducing him to other godly men and women. Help him see the difference between the lifestyle of the non-believer, of the carnal believer and of one who has made Christ his Lord.

Teach him how to walk in the control and power of the Holy Spirit. To emphasize Christian living without a proper understanding of the personal ministry of the Holy Spirit will only lead to frustration, legalism, and defeat.

The most liberating truth you can teach your disciple is the concept of Spiritual Breathing: how to exhale spiritually by confessing sin and how to inhale spiritually by appropriating the control and cleansing of God's Spirit by faith. (See appendix C, "How to Walk in the Spirit.")

Help him understand the importance of reading the Word of God regularly, and of studying it, memorizing it and meditating on its truths daily. The Bible is God's holy, inspired Word to man. It is impossible to become a mature disciple without an understanding of God's Word. Help your disciple realize that every spiritual and practical problem he will ever encounter has an answer in the Word of God, directly or indirectly.

Teach him the importance of Christian fellowship, especially through the local church and through a small group Bible study. Christians need each other for encouragement, caring, learning from one another, and accountability to each other. Encourage your disciple to be baptized and to join a caring, Bible-teaching fellowship of believers. Baptism is part of one's commitment to Christ that is often overlooked in the follow-up process. In the Great Commission, Jesus said, "As you go making disciples, baptize them and teach them." It is important for believers to be baptized as an act of obedience, and as public testimony of their commitment to Christ.

Emphasize the importance of love. Read the great passages in the Scriptures that emphasize love, especially 1 Corinthians 13, and ask God to demonstrate that quality in your own life as an example. As Jesus reminds us in John 13:35, "By this all men will know that you are My disciples, if you have love for one another." Together, study the Transferable Concept, *How to Love by Faith.*

Teach your disciple how to be a good steward of everything with which God has entrusted him. We must never forget that everything we have is a gift from God. Help your disciple to understand the principle of honoring God in the way he uses his mind, body and spirit, as well as his time, talent and treasure. Help him plan and use his time wisely; encourage him to develop his abilities and utilize them in the Lord's work; and help him learn to use his money wisely and to lay up treasures in heaven.

Teach him how to witness by inviting him to go witnessing with you. It is not enough to explain all the methods, techniques and strategies; it is not enough to have him learn to use the Four Spiritual Laws. Just as one learns to pray by praying, so one learns to witness by witnessing. Show him how to write a three-minute testimony (chapter 7), then help him polish and rehearse it. After he has observed you in two or three witnessing situations, ask him to handle the next one.

Finally, *impart a vision for the fulfillment of the Great Commission of our Lord and Savior.* For example, if your disciple is a student, plan together how he can help spread the gospel in classes, dorms or other segments of the campus population. If your disciple is married, share how he and his spouse can win and disciple the couples in their neighborhood for Christ. If you are discipling a businessman, show him how he can start Bible studies and evangelistic luncheons to help reach others in the business community. These types of outreaches are being conducted successfully, every day, by Christians who are compelled by the love of Jesus Christ to share "the greatest news ever announced." And while you impart a vision for your disciples' personal spheres of influence, help them understand their privilege and responsibility for helping to reach the entire world as well (Acts 1:8).

WHAT ABOUT FAILURES?

Often, I have shed tears of heartache and sorrow over men and women into whose lives I have poured much time and prayer, only to have them drift away to dishonor the Lord. Then the Lord reminded me that they were His responsibility. He reminded me of how

Christ's Parable of the Sower teaches that not all seed falls on good soil. Some people fall away. While it can be disappointing, I have learned that I need to keep on trusting God and not be discouraged in my efforts to win and build men and women for Christ. Just as successful witnessing is simply taking the initiative to share Christ in the power of the Holy Spirit, and leaving the results to God, so:

Successful follow-up is simply taking the initiative to build disciples in the power of the Holy Spirit, and leaving the results to God.

Take follow-up and discipling seriously—they go hand-in-glove with successful witnessing. Never forsake a witnessing opportunity just because you don't feel you would be able to follow up on someone—you can always network a new believer to a pastor or another Christian who will work with him.

Likewise, never forsake follow-up and disciple-building with a new believer when the opportunity is there. Not only will you be helping a person grow into a mature, caring member of the Body of Christ, but you will also experience the indescribable blessing of being God's chosen workman in the process.

SUMMARY

●It is essential to begin follow-up with the new Christian within forty-eight hours of his conversion.

●If the new believer does not live near you, commit to several telephone calls and/or letters to help him begin his Christian growth. Network him to a good church in his area, and write the pastor asking him to take the initiative to invite your friend to church activities.

●Take time to answer the new Christian's questions and concerns. Utilize the Transferable Concepts series and encourage him to write his answers to the study questions.

●Encourage your friend to become involved in a caring, Bible-teaching church, and in a small-group Bible study.

●Pray daily for your disciple.

●Model the attributes of Spirit-controlled living in your daily walk.

FOR REFLECTION AND ACTION

1. If you received Christ as an adult, reflect on the first twenty-four hours after you became a Christian. What thoughts went through your mind? What doubts and questions? How did your friends and loved ones respond?

2. Visit your Christian bookstore and examine the Transferable Concepts. (Or, order directly from Here's Life Publishers. See instructions in appendix E.) Obtain a small quantity of *How to Be Sure You Are a Christian* and *How to Experience God's Love and Forgiveness* and study them for future reference and for sharing with others whom you want to encourage in Christian growth.

3. Do you know any new Christians right now (whether or not you led them to the Lord) who would benefit from your willingness to disciple them? Ask them if they would like to meet with you to discuss the possibility. If they agree, begin utilizing the principles of this chapter as you meet regularly with them.

4. Is there someone you have led to Christ or discipled in the past, with whom you've lost contact? Ask God if He wants you to take the initiative to get back in touch, restore the friendship, and possibly continue the discipling process.

5. Be sure at all times, but *especially* in follow-up

and discipling, that you are filled with the Holy Spirit—
that the Lord is on the throne of your life. Keep your
motives centered on loving and honoring the Lord in
everything you do.

*By your obedience to God's command,
you can influence generations to come*

❧12❧

"YOU JUST NEVER KNOW..."

Inauguration Day, 1981. It was a bitter cold, January morning in Washington, D.C., but one just doesn't turn down an invitation to such a special event. I felt honored to be invited to watch Ronald Reagan take the oath of office and to participate in the other activities of the week.

It has been my privilege over the years to interact with many Washington officials, and many have given their lives to Christ. But it has been just as great a privilege to interact with lay men and women, cab drivers, hotel maids, and others with whom the Lord has brought me in contact.

I have shared honestly with you how witnessing situations are not always "easy" or natural for me. But I have found that, as I obey God out of my love and gratitude for Him, He has blessed my initiative and indeed enriched my life with a deep inner happiness that could only come from helping a fellow human being trust the Lord Jesus.

One of our country's most highly regarded senators

171

was the chairman of the Inauguration Day's events, and as he emceed the ceremonies my mind drifted back through the years to recall several other occasions in which God had worked in people's lives . . .

I thought of the time the dean of students at Willamette University had invited me to speak to the student body and other student groups on campus. He was a faithful churchgoer, and I assumed he was a Christian because of the nature of his invitation to me. While on campus for several days, I had the privilege of helping a number of students receive Christ—and every time one did, I asked him to go tell the dean, confident that he would be pleased.

I encouraged these new Christians to form a Bible class, and they asked the dean to be their sponsor. He told me later that one day, while visiting one of their Bible classes, "I was so overwhelmed at the change in their lives that I decided to receive Christ, too. I had been a church member but I wasn't a Christian." So he went home, got on his knees, and invited the Lord into his life . . .

I remembered the hotel elevator operator in Boston. The hotel was one of those grand old palaces, the kind where the elevators required a full-time operator. I was in town for a few days of training conferences, and I met her after a long, full day of meetings.

I guessed her to be in her late sixties. She looked bored and tired, and her eyes stared blankly at the floor numbers as we ascended past each floor.

"You go up and down all day long," I ventured.

"Yes," she sighed. "All day."

"You know, one day you'll go up and never come down, if you're ready. Are you ready?"

She knew what I was talking about. "No, I'm not."

"Would you like to be?"

She turned toward me on her stool, and for the first time her eyes met mine. "Why, yes. Yes, I would."

Even after all these years, it's amazing to me how God prepares people. He had prepared this woman's heart for His message of love and hope. I pulled a copy of the Four Spiritual Laws booklet from my pocket.

"Why don't you take this home and read it. There's a little prayer in the booklet, and it tells you what to do. I'll see you tomorrow and we can talk some more."

God always works mightily through His Word, and He used the Four Spiritual Laws booklet that night to change not only this woman's life, but another life as well. The next day, I entered her elevator and asked her what had happened.

Her smile made her look twenty years younger. "Well, I live in a crowded, one-room apartment with my mother, so the only place I could find privacy was the bathroom. I went into the bathroom, read the booklet, and I got on my knees and I asked Jesus into my heart.

"Then I took it and read it to my mother [who must have been at least eighty-five years old]. She said, 'That's what I want to do, too!' and she asked Jesus into her heart. Now we both know where we're going— we're going up!"

I recalled that first meeting of students in our home at UCLA, the night after I spoke in "the house of beautiful women" sorority. One of the women brought her boyfriend, the star halfback of the UCLA football team, and he approached me privately after I had explained how to receive Christ.

"I've never heard anything like this before," he said. "I want to talk with you some more."

The following Sunday, aching from a bone-crunching victory on the football field the day before, he accompanied Vonette and me to church with his girlfriend. Then, as Vonette and Marilyn prepared lunch, he told me, "You know, all my life I've played football so I could be All-American—but it occurred to me as you spoke this week that if I broke a leg and couldn't play anymore, I wouldn't have anything to live for. I realize that I need God."

So we got on our knees and prayed. As we got up, he smiled and announced, "Now I want to be an All-American for God."

He was an All-American on the gridiron for three years at UCLA. And during that time, he was confidently sharing Christ with his teammates and other students, and leading many of them to the Lord . . .

I remembered the motel maid in Florida. As I was rushing from my room to meet one of the prominent men in the city, the Lord impressed me that here, right before me, was someone just as precious in His sight.

As I talked with her, her distress poured out. She felt unloved and unappreciated by her family. "No one really cares about me," she lamented. "My employer doesn't care, my family doesn't care, nobody cares."

I told her how God cares for her, loves her, and offers a wonderful plan for her. When we read through the Four Spiritual Laws, she invited Christ into her life and smiled at me through her tears. Later that day, the executive received Christ, too . . .

Over the years, wherever I have traveled, I have asked Christians two questions. *What is the most important thing that has ever happened to you?* Invariably, they answer, "Receiving Jesus Christ as my personal Savior and Lord." The second question: *What, then, is the most important thing you can do in life to leave a positive mark on society?* Invariably, a light goes on in the eyes of my fellow believers. "Tell others the good news—that Christ died for their sins and offers them abundant, eternal life."

It has indeed been a privilege to reach out through my shyness and introduce others to our Savior. From the cab driver to the U.S. senator, from the blue-collar worker to the influential businessman, all are equal and precious in God's sight and all need Jesus Christ.

My mind came back to the inauguration ceremony as I realized what was happening. That dean of students who received Christ at Willamette University years ago was to become a U.S. senator, the same distinguished gentleman who was emceeing the ceremonies on this January morning. In the intervening years, this devout Christian has honored me by calling me one of his "spiritual fathers."

The senator was at this moment introducing one of the nation's most influential pastors, who would give the invocation. This pastor was that All-American halfback at UCLA who had trusted Christ with me in our living room. He has been the President's pastor for more than twenty-five years.

Vonette and I were guests of another U.S. senator and his wife. Many analysts have named him a "rising star" in Congress. A few years before, while a congressman in the House of Representatives, he had received Christ through the Four Spiritual Laws. Now, he was a bold, intelligent voice for Christianity among our nation's policymakers. His wife had received Christ as her Savior and Lord through the witness of one of our staff women in Washington, D. C., and was now involved in leading women's Bible studies for congressional wives.

As I thought about these people, and of the others the Lord had brought into His kingdom through our ministry, the thought occurred to me: *You just never know, when you take the initiative to share Christ, what will become of it.*

Some may turn you down outright.

Others may express some interest, but not feel "ready."

Others may receive Christ with you, but you won't have opportunity for follow-up.

But God loves each of these people even more than you do.

He is not willing that any should perish.

And when you've been faithful and done your part,

you can leave the results to Him.

Just as He has with that elevator operator, and with those two senators, and with that influential pastor, and with that senator's wife, He may use your obedience in sharing Him to influence generations to come.

All He expects of us is obedience. To share openly, lovingly, without reservation, the greatest news ever announced:

God loves you,
and offers a wonderful plan for your life.

APPENDIX A
THE VAN DUSEN LETTER

This letter was written to a prominent business acquaintance who had requested information on how to become a Christian. The name Dr. Van Dusen is fictitious. Over the years, many millions of copies of this letter have been distributed around the world in most major languages as an evangelistic tool with remarkable results. May we suggest that you order copies of this letter for widespread distribution.

Dr. Randolph Van Dusen
Groton Manor
Islip, Long Island, New York

Dear Dr. Van Dusen:

Cordial greetings from sunny California! Thank you for your recent letter requesting additional information. The warm expression of your desire to know more about Jesus Christ, the Lord, encourages me to explain briefly the basic facts concerning the Christian life.

First, I would like to have you think of the Christian life as a great adventure, for Jesus said, "I am come that they might have life, and that they might have it more abundantly" (John 10:10).

Second, I want you to know that God loves us and has a wonderful, exciting plan for every life. We are not creatures of chance, brought into the world for a meaningless, miserable existence; but rather, we are children of destiny, created for lives of purpose and joyful service to God and our fellow man. Any student knows that there are definite laws in the physical realm that are inviolate; just so, there are definite spiritual laws that govern our spiritual lives.

Since man is the highest known form of life, and since there is a purpose for everything else, does it not make sense that there is a plan for us? If God created us for a purpose, does it not logically follow that that purpose somehow, somewhere, has been revealed? Would this One who created us then leave us to shift for ourselves? All evidence would demonstrate the contrary. How, then, can man know God's plan?

There are many religions, and most of them have their "sacred writings." Yet, when these are studied in an objective manner, it soon becomes very evident that the Old and New Testaments of the Bible differ vastly from the others. Though there is much good in the writings of these various religions, it soon becomes obvious that they in no way compare with the sacred Scriptures upon which Christianity is based.

While studying for three years in two of our country's leading seminaries under some of the world's greatest scholars, it was proven conclusively to me that, in a unique and special way, God has spoken to men through the writings of the Bible.

Every man is seeking happiness, but the Bible says that true happiness can be found only through God's way. Let me explain simply what this way is. The Bible says that God is holy and that man is sinful. There is a great chasm between them. Man is continually trying to find God (see Diagram 1). From the most ignorant savage to the most brilliant professor on the university campus, man is trying to find God and the abundant life through his own efforts. Through the various philosophies and religions of history, man has tried to cross this chasm to find God and a life of purpose and happiness. Man can no more bridge this chasm than he can jump across the Grand Canyon flatfooted, or climb to heaven on a six-foot ladder. The Bible explains that this is impossible because God is holy and righteous, and man is sinful. Man was created to have fellowship with God, but because of his own stubborn self-will and disobedience, man chose to go his own independent way and fellowship was broken. That is what the Bible calls sin.

Pull the plug of a floor lamp out of its wall socket; contact with the electrical current is broken and the light goes out. This is comparable to what happens to man when fellowship with God is broken. The Bible says, "For all have sinned and come short of the glory of God" (Romans 3:23); "For the wages of sin is death; but the gift of God is eternal life through Jesus Christ our Lord" (Romans 6:23).

You will observe that I am not saying that sin is a matter of getting drunk, committing murder, being immoral, etc. These are only the results of sin. You say, "What are the symptoms of a life separated from God?" In addition to some of the grosser sins, there are, for some people, worry, irritability, lack of purpose in life, no goal, no power, no real interest in living, utter boredom, inferiority complex, frustration, desire to escape reality, and fear of death. These and many others are evidence that man is cut off from the only One who can give him the power to live the abundant life.

St. Augustine, one of the greatest philosophers and theologians of all time, said, "Thou hast made us for Thyself, O God, and our hearts are restless until they find their rest in Thee."

Pascal, the great physicist and philosopher, more recently said, as he described the longing in the human heart, "There is a God-shaped vacuum in the heart of each man, which cannot be satisfied by any created thing but only by God, the Creator, made known through Jesus Christ."

Now, if God has a plan for us, a plan which includes a full and abundant life, and all of man's efforts to find God are futile, we must turn to the Bible to discover God's way.

The Bible tells us that "God so loved the world, that He gave His only begotten Son, that whosoever believeth in Him should not perish, but have everlasting life" (John 3:16). In other words, this great chasm between God and man cannot be bridged by man's effort, but only by God's effort through His Son, Jesus Christ. Let me call your attention to the fact that we cannot know God through good works. "For by grace are ye saved through faith; and that not of yourselves: it is the gift of God: not of works, lest any man should boast" (Ephesians 2:8,9). Good works will follow an acceptance of God's gift, as an expression of our gratitude.

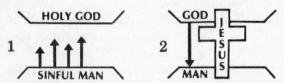

Religion and philosophy have been defined as man's best attempts to find God. Christianity has been defined as God's best effort to find man.

Now, who is this person, Jesus Christ, that He, more than anyone who has ever lived, has the power to bridge this chasm between a Holy God and sinful man? (See Diagram 2.) By way of review, Jesus of Nazareth was conceived by the Holy Ghost and born of the Virgin Mary almost 2,000 years ago. Hundreds of years before, great prophets of Israel foretold His coming. The Old Testament, which was written by many individuals over a period of 1,500 years, contains over 300 references to His coming. At the age of 30, He began His public ministry. Space will not allow for details except to say that, in the three years following, He gave man the formula for a full and abundant life, and for a life to come.

The life Jesus led, the miracles He performed, the words He spoke, His death on the cross, His resurrection, His ascent to heaven, all point to the fact that He was not a mere man, but more than man. He Himself claimed to be God. "I and My Father are One" (John 10:30); and "he that hath seen Me hath seen the Father" (John 14:9).

The late Arnold Toynbee, one of the most eminent historians of our century, has given more space to Jesus of Nazareth than to any other six great men who have ever lived, including Mohammed, Buddha, Caesar, Napoleon and George Washington.

The Encyclopedia Britannica gives 20,000 words to Jesus. Thinking men of all lands and religions, who have the opportunity to investigate the evidence, will agree that Jesus is the greatest personality the world has ever known. Consider statements made by these distinguished writers:

●"Jesus Christ is the outstanding personality of all time . . . no other teacher—Jewish, Christian, Buddhist, Mohammedan—is still a teacher whose teaching is such a guidepost for the world we live in. Other teachers may have something basic for an Oriental, an Arab, or an Occidental; but every act and word of Jesus has value for all of us. He became the Light of the World. Why shouldn't I, a Jew, be proud of that?"

Sholem Asch

●"If ever man was God, or God man, Jesus Christ was both."

Lord Byron

●"No revolution that has ever taken place in society can be compared to that which has been produced by the words of Jesus Christ."

Mark Hopkins

●"The greatest revolution ever was Jesus Christ Himself; not His ideas, not His teaching, not His moral principles, but He Himself; for nothing is greater, more revolutionary, and more unbelievable than the gospel of the crucified, resurrected and glorified God who is to come again to judge the living and the dead."

Charles Malick

●"I have read in Plato and Cicero sayings that are very wise and very beautiful; but I have never read in either of them: 'Come unto me all that labour and are heavy laden.'"

St. Augustine

●"If Shakespeare should come into this room, we would rise; but if Jesus Christ should come in, we would all kneel."

Charles Lamb

It is important to consider that Jesus Christ claimed to be God. He claimed to be the author of a new way of life. Historically, we know that wherever His message has gone, new life, new hope and new purpose for living have resulted. Either Jesus of Nazareth was who He claimed to be, the Son of God, the Savior of mankind, or He was the greatest impostor the world has ever known. If His claims were false, more good has resulted from a lie than has ever been accomplished by the truth. Does it not make sense that this person (whom most people knowing the facts consider the greatest teacher, the greatest example, the greatest leader the world has ever known), would be, as He Himself claimed to be, and as the Bible tells us that He is, the one person who could bridge the chasm between God and man?

You will remember Romans 6:23, to which I referred, "For the wages of sin is death; but the gift of God is eternal life through Jesus Christ our Lord." As you study the religions and philosophies of the world, you will find no provision for man's sin, apart from the cross of Jesus Christ. The Bible says that without the shedding of blood there is no remission or forgiveness of sin (Hebrews 9:22). In Acts 4:12, we are told, "Neither is there salvation in any other: for there is none other name under heaven given among men, whereby we must be saved."

Jesus said, "I am the way, the truth, and the life: no man cometh unto the Father, but by Me" (John 14:6). Let me quote to you what Jesus said to a man who came to Him for counsel. They talked, even as we have talked. Turn to the third chapter of John's Gospel and read the first eight verses. First, notice who Nicodemus was.

Nicodemus was a Pharisee, a ruler of the Jews, one of the great religious leaders of his day. We find that, so far as the law was concerned, he was above reproach. He was moral and ethical. He was so eager to please God that he prayed seven times a day. He went to the synagogue to worship God three times a day. Yet he saw in the life of Jesus something which he had never experienced himself; there was a different quality of life altogether. You will note that Nicodemus approached Jesus by saying, "'Rabbi, we know that Thou art a teacher come from God; for no man can do these miracles that Thou doest, except God be with Him.' Jesus answered and said unto him, 'Verily, verily, I say unto thee, except a man be born again, he cannot see the kingdom of God.' Nicodemus saith unto Him, 'How can a man be born when he is old? Can he enter the second time into his mother's womb and be born?' Jesus answered, 'Verily, verily, I say unto thee, except a man be born of water and of the Spirit, he cannot enter the kingdom of God. That which is born of the flesh is flesh; and that which is born of the Spirit is spirit'" (John 3:2-6).

Consider, for example, a caterpillar crawling in the dust—an ugly, hairy worm. One day this worm weaves about its body a cocoon. From this cocoon there emerges a beautiful butterfly. We do not understand fully what has taken place. We realize only that where once an ugly worm crawled in the dust, now a beautiful butterfly soars in the heavens. So it is in the lives of Christians. Where once we lived on the lowest level as sinful, egocentric individuals, we now dwell on the highest plane, experiencing full and abundant lives as children of God. An individual becomes a Christian through a spiritual birth. In other words, God is Spirit and we cannot communicate with Him until we become spiritual creatures. (This is what takes place when Jesus comes to live in our lives.) Without His indwelling presence, we cannot communicate with God; we know nothing of His plan for our lives; the Word of God is a dull, uninteresting book. However, when Jesus comes into our lives and we become Spirit-controlled, we love to be with Christians, we love to read the Word of God and we want our lives to count for Him. Just suppose, for the sake of illustration, that we are sitting in a room and we know that there are a number of television programs available to us. We are looking and listening, yet we cannot see the images or hear the voices. What is needed? An instrument—a television set. The moment that we move the television set into the room and turn the dial, we can hear a voice and see an image. So it is when Christ comes into our lives. He is our divine instrument, tuning us in to God, making known God's will and love for our lives.

Basically, the only thing that separates an individual from God—and thus from His love and forgiveness—is his own self-will. (Please do not think me presumptuous. I do not wish to embarrass you by encouraging you to do anything that you are reluctant to do. However, because you expressed such genuine interest in knowing more about these matters when we talked face to face, I am taking the liberty, as one who sincerely cares, by encouraging you to enter into this relationship with Christ today—now!)

Well do I remember that night several years ago when, alone in my room, I knelt to surrender my will for the will of Christ. While in prayer, I invited Him to enter the "door" of my life, forgive my sin and take His rightful place on the throne. I must confess that there was no great emotional response, as some have—actually none at all—but, true to His promise, Christ came in; and gradually, like the blooming of a lovely rose, the beauty and fragrance of His presence became real to me. Though in my spiritual ignorance as a nonbeliever I had considered myself to be perfectly happy and fulfilled with life, He gave me a new and genuine quality of life altogether—a promise of abundant life fulfilled in ways too numerous to mention.

God loves you so much that He gave His only begotten Son to die on the cross for your sins; and Jesus Christ, the Son of God, loved you enough to die on the cross for you. Here He is, the greatest leader, the greatest teacher, the greatest example the world has ever known. But more than this, He is the Son of God, your Savior. Can you think of anyone whom you would rather follow?

Perhaps you are asking, "Suppose I invite Christ into my life and nothing happens? Maybe the Lord will not hear me." May I assure you that you can trust Christ. He promised to come in. He does not lie. A chemist going into a laboratory to work an experiment knows that, by following the Table of Chemical Valence, he will get the desired results. The mathematician knows that the multiplication table is tried and dependable, and that the law of gravity is inviolate. Just so, the laws of the spiritual realm are definite and true, and when God, who created all things and established the laws that govern all things, says that He will enter and change your life, you may accept this promise without question.

However, a word of caution is in order. Do not put undue emphasis on feelings. There must be a balanced emphasis on fact (intellect), faith (trust, involving the will), and feeling (involving the emotions). Meditate on the following verses:

Jesus said, "Behold, I stand at the door, and knock: if any man hear My voice and open the door, I will come in to him, and will sup with him, and he with Me" (Revelation 3:20). "I am come that they might have life, and they might have it more abundantly" (John 10:10). He has come to forgive your sins. He has come to bring peace and purpose to your life.

Our lives are filled with many activities, such as business, travel, finances, social life and home life, often with no real purpose or meaning. Jesus knocks at the heart's door, seeking entrance. He will not force Himself. Jesus wants to come into your life and make harmony out of discord—to create meaning and purpose where now there is something lacking. He wants to forgive your sin and bridge the gulf between you and God. He does not want to enter your life as a guest, but He wants to control your life as Lord and Master.

Self-Controlled Life

There is a throne in each heart. All of these years, your ego has been on the throne. Now Christ waits for you to invite Him to be on the throne. You must step down and relinquish the authority of your life to Him.

Christ-Controlled Life

You can see from this simple diagram how, when Christ becomes Lord of your life, He becomes Lord of every activity, which, as you can see, makes for a harmonious life. Is it not better to be controlled by the infinite, loving God who created you and suffered for you than to continue under the control of finite self?

The great difference Christ makes may be seen in the realm of marriage. Though one out of every two marriages ends in divorce, surveys indicate that in Christian marriages where the family practice of Bible study and prayer is observed daily, there is only one divorce in more than 1,000 marriages. Why the difference? The answer is simple. The ego of the husband reacts against the ego of the wife, or vice versa. Friction and discord result. Yet when Christ is on the throne of each life, there can be no discord—only harmony—as He does not war against Himself.

In John 1:12, we are told, "But as many as received Him, to them gave He power to become the sons of God, even to them that believe on His name." "And this is the record, that God hath given to us eternal life, and this life is in His Son. He that hath the Son hath life; and he that hath not the Son of God hath not life" (1 John 5:11,12). (Speaking of life, few people give serious thought to the fact that we must one day die. The Scripture reminds us that "it is appointed unto men once to die, and after this the judgment" [Hebrews 9:27]. Christ prepares men for death as well as for life, and a man is not ready to live until he is ready to die.)

"Therefore if any man be in Christ, he is a new creature: old things are passed away; behold, all things are become new" (2 Corinthians 5:17).

Will you not sincerely invite the Lord Jesus into your heart, and surrender your will completely to Him, right now? We can talk with God through prayer. Why not find a quiet place where you can kneel or bow reverently in God's presence and ask Christ to come into your heart. In your prayer, you can say something like this:

"Lord Jesus, I need You. Thank You for dying on the cross for my sins. I open the door of my life and receive You as my Savior and Lord. Thank You for forgiving my sins and giving me eternal life. Take control of the throne of my life. Make me the kind of person You want me to be."

To invite Christ into your life is absolutely the most important decision that you will ever make; and when you do so, several wonderful things will happen:

1. Christ will actually come to live in your heart.

2. Your sins will be forgiven.

3. You will truly become a child of God.

4. You are assured of heaven.

5. Your life becomes a great adventure, as God reveals His plan and purpose and as you continue to live in faith and obedience.

Did you ask Christ into your heart? Were you sincere? Where is He right now? In the event that you are disappointed because there may have been no great emotional experience—though some may indeed know this immediate joy—I want to remind you again that a Christian must place his faith in the Word of God, not in feelings; for emotions come and go, but the Word of God is trustworthy and true. Christ promised to enter when you opened the door. He does not lie. Meditate again on the truth of Revelation 3:20; John 1:12; 1 John 5:11-13; 2 Corinthians 5:17. Take time right now to thank God for what has happened to you as you have prayed.

Since you have never been satisfied with mediocrity in your business, you will certainly not want to be an ordinary Christian. It costs us nothing to become Christians, although it cost God His own dear Son to give us this privilege. But it will cost us both time and effort to be the kind of Christian which God would have us be. For obvious reasons, a Christian should be a better businessman, father, husband, mother, student, or whatever.

Here is a suggestion that will enable you to grow quickly in the Christian life, illustrated by a simple little word . . . GROWTH:

G Go to God in prayer daily.

R Read God's Word daily—begin with the Gospel of John.

O Obey God, moment by moment.

W Witness for Christ by your life and words.

T Trust God for every detail of your life.

H Holy Spirit—allow Him to control and empower your daily life and actions (Galatians 5:16,17; Acts 1:8).

In Hebrews 10:25, we are admonished to "forsake not the assembling of ourselves together. . ." Several logs burn brightly together; put one aside on the cold hearth and the fire goes out. So it is with you and your relationship to other Christians. If you do not belong to a church, do not wait to be invited. Take the initiative; call the pastor of a nearby church where Christ is honored and the Bible is preached. Make plans to start next Sunday and to attend each week. Be assured of my love and prayers as you make this all important decision. We shall be looking forward to hearing from you soon.

Sincerely yours,

Bill Bright

William R. Bright, President

APPENDIX B

HOW TO BE FILLED WITH THE SPIRIT

Condensed from the Transferable Concept by Bill Bright

Most Christians live in self-imposed spiritual poverty because they don't know how to appropriate from God the spiritual resources which are already theirs.

During the Depression a man named Yates owned a sheep ranch in West Texas. Because he did not earn enough money to make his ranching operation pay, Mr. Yates was in danger of losing his ranch. His family, like many others, had to live on government subsidy.

Day after day, as Mr. Yates grazed his sheep over those rolling West Texas hills, he was greatly troubled over how to meet his financial obligations. Then a seismographic crew from an oil company came into the area and informed Mr. Yates that they felt there might be oil on his land. They asked permission to drill a wildcat test well and he signed a lease contract.

At 1,115 feet they struck a huge oil reserve. The first well came in at 80,000 barrels a day. Many subsequent wells were more than twice as large. And Mr. Yates owned it all! The day he purchased the land he received the oil and mineral rights. Yet, he had been living on relief—a multimillionaire living in poverty. The problem? He did not know the oil was there. He owned it, but he did not *possess* it.

I do not know of a better illustration of the Christian life than this. The moment we become children of God through faith in Christ, we become heirs of God, and all of His divine supernatural resources are made available to us. Everything we need—including wisdom, love, power—to be men and women of God and to be fruitful witnesses for Christ is available to us. But most Christians continue to live in self-imposed spiritual poverty because they do not know how to appropriate from God those spiritual resources which are already theirs.

It is useless to try to live in our own power the kind of life God has commanded us to live. Our strength must come from the Lord! The Holy Spirit came to enable us to know Christ. When we receive Christ into our lives, we experience a new birth, and are indwelt by the Spirit. The Holy Spirit enables us to live and share the abundant life which Jesus promised to all who trust Him.

LACK OF FAITH

Many Christians are not filled, controlled and empowered with the Spirit because of a lack of knowledge. Unbelief keeps others from experiencing the abundant life. There are still other Christians who may have been exposed to the truth concerning the person and ministry of the Holy Spirit but who, for various reasons, have never been able to comprehend the love of God. They are afraid of Him. They simply do not trust Him.

Suppose, when my two sons were young, they had greeted me with these words: "Daddy, we love you and have decided that we will do anything you want us to do from now on as long as we live." What do you think would have been my attitude?

If I had responded to their expression of trust in me as many believe God will respond when they surrender their lives to Him, I would have taken my sons by the shoulders, shaken them, glared at them sternly and said, "I have just been waiting for this! I am going to make you regret this decision for as long as you live. I am going to take all the fun out of your lives—give away your toys and make you do all the things you do not like to do."

Many people believe this is the way God will respond when they say, "Lord, I surrender the control of my life to You." They do not understand how much God loves them. Do you know what I would do if my sons came to me with such a greeting? I would put my arms around them and say, "I love you, too, and I deeply appreciate this expression of your love for me. It is the greatest gift which you could give me and I want to do everything in my power to merit your love and trust."

Is God any less loving and concerned for His children? No, He has proved over and over again that He is a loving God—our heavenly Father who cares deeply for His children. He is worthy of our trust.

FILLED BY FAITH

How can one be filled with the Holy Spirit? We are filled with the Spirit by faith. We received Christ by faith. We walk by faith. Everything we receive from God, from the moment of our spiritual birth until we die, is by faith.

You do not have to beg God to fill you with His Holy Spirit. You do not have to barter with Him by fasting, weeping, or pleading. For a long time I fasted, prayed and cried out to God for His fullness. Then one day I discovered from the Scriptures that "the just shall live by faith."[1] *We do not earn God's fullness. We receive it by faith.*

Suppose you want to cash a check for a hundred dollars. Would you go to the bank where you have several thousand dollars on deposit, place the check on the counter, get down on your knees, and say, "Oh, please, Mr. Teller, cash my check"? No, that is not the way you cash a check. You simply go in faith, place the check on the counter, and wait for the money which is already yours. Then you thank the teller and go on your way.

Millions of Christians are begging God, as I once did, for something which is already available—just waiting to be appropriated by faith. They are seeking some kind of emotional experience, not realizing that such an attitude on their part is an insult to God—a denial of faith, by which we please God. In Hebrews 11:6 we are told, "Without faith it is impossible to please God..."

HEART PREPARATION

Though you are filled with the Holy Spirit by faith and faith alone, it is important to recognize that several factors contribute to preparing your heart for the filling of the Spirit.

First, you must hunger and thirst after God and desire to be controlled and empowered by His Holy Spirit. We have the promise of our Savior, "Blessed are those who hunger and thirst after righteousness, for they shall be filled."[2]

Second, be willing to surrender your life to Christ in accordance with Paul's admonition in Romans 12:1,2: "And so, dear brothers, I plead with you to give your bodies to God. Let them be a living sacrifice, holy—the kind He can accept. When you think of what He has done for you, is this too much to ask? Don't copy the behavior and customs of this world, but be a new and different person with a fresh newness in all you do and think. Then you will learn from your own experience how His ways will really satisfy you" (TLB).

Third, confess every known sin which the Holy Spirit brings to your remembrance and experience the cleansing and forgiveness which God promises in 1 John 1:9: "But if we confess our sins to Him, He can be depended on to forgive us and to cleanse us from every wrong. And it is perfectly proper for God to do this for us because Christ died to wash away our sins" (TLB).

COMMAND AND PROMISE

There are two very important words to remember. The first is *command.* In Ephesians 5:18 God commands us to be filled: "Be not drunk with wine, wherein is excess, but be filled with the Spirit" (KJV). Not to be controlled and empowered by the Holy Spirit is disobedience. The other word is *promise*—a promise that makes the command possible: "This is the confidence which we have before Him, that, *if we ask anything according to His will, He hears us. And if we know that He hears us in whatever we ask, we know that we have the requests which we have asked from Him.*"[3]

Now, is it God's will for you to be filled, controlled and empowered by the Holy Spirit? Of course it is His will—for it is His command. Right now, then, you can ask God the Holy Spirit to fill you—not because you deserve to be filled, but on the basis of His command and promise.

If you are a Christian, the Holy Spirit already dwells within you. Therefore, you do not need to invite Him to come into your life. The moment you received Christ, the Holy Spirit not only came to indwell you, but He imparted to you spiritual life, causing you to be born anew as a child of God. The Holy Spirit also baptized you into the body of Christ. In 1 Corinthians 12:13, Paul explains, "For by one Spirit we are all baptized into one body."

There is but one *indwelling* of the Holy Spirit, one *rebirth* of the Holy Spirit, and one *baptism* of the Holy Spirit—all of which occur the moment you receive Christ. There are many *fillings*, as is made clear in

Ephesians 5:18. In the Greek language in which the New Testament was originally written, the meaning is clearer than in most English translations. This command of God means to *be constantly and continually filled, controlled and empowered with the Holy Spirit as a way of life.*

If you wish to be technical, you do not need to pray to be filled with the Holy Spirit, as there is no place in Scripture where we are told to pray for the filling of the Holy Spirit. *We are filled by faith.* However, since the object of our faith is God and His Word, I suggest that you pray to be filled with the Holy Spirit as an expression of your faith in God's command and in His promise. You are not filled because you pray, but because by faith you trust God to fill you with His Spirit in response to your faith.

Have you met God's conditions? Do you hunger and thirst after righteousness? Have you confessed every known sin in your life? Do you sincerely desire to be controlled and empowered by the Holy Spirit, to make Jesus Christ the Lord of your life? If so, I invite you to bow and pray a prayer of faith right now. Claim the fullness of the Holy Spirit by faith:

"Dear Father, I need You. I acknowledge that I have been in control of my life and that, as a result, I have sinned against You. I thank You that You have forgiven my sins through Christ's death on the cross for me. I now invite Christ to take control of the throne of my life. Fill me with the Holy Spirit as You commanded me to be filled and as You promised in Your Word that You would do if I asked in faith. I pray this in the authority of the name of the Lord Jesus Christ. As an expression of my faith, I now thank You for filling me with Your Holy Spirit and for taking control of my life."

If this prayer expressed the desire of your heart, and you met God's conditions of heart preparation, you can be sure that God has answered you. You are now filled with the Holy Spirit whether you "feel" like it or not. Do not depend on emotions—we are to live by faith, not feelings.

You can begin this very moment to draw upon the vast, inexhaustible resources of the Holy Spirit to enable you to live a holy life, and to share the claims of the Lord Jesus and His love and forgiveness with men everywhere. Remember that being filled with the Holy Spirit is a way of life. We are commanded to be constantly controlled by the Holy Spirit. Thank Him for the fullness of His Spirit as you begin each day and continue to invite Him to control your life moment by moment. This is your heritage as a child of God.

1. Galatians 3:11 (KJV); 2. Matthew 5:6; 3. 1 John 5:14,15.

APPENDIX C

HOW TO WALK IN THE SPIRIT

Condensed from the Transferable Concept
by Bill Bright

Once you've given Christ control of the "throne" of your life, what's to keep SELF from climbing back up on that throne and sabotaging God's loving guidance?

"Since I have learned how to walk in the fullness and power of the Spirit, the Christian life has become a great adventure for me," said a medical doctor after completing his third Lay Institute for Evangelism. "Now, I want everyone to experience this same exciting adventure with Christ."

Would you like to know how to experience a full, abundant, purposeful and fruitful life? You can! If you have been living in spiritual defeat— wondering if there is any validity to the Christian life—I have good news. There is great hope for you!

The Christian life, properly understood, is not complex nor difficult. As a matter of fact, the Christian life is so simple that we stumble over the very simplicity of it, yet it is so difficult that no one can live it! This paradox occurs because the Christian life is a *super-*

natural life. The only one who can live it is our Lord
Jesus Christ. It is only as we consistently abide in Him
and walk in His Spirit that we will experience the
abundant life with all that Christ means the Christian
life to be.

How to walk in the Spirit through the practice of
what I like to call "Spiritual Breathing" is a simple-
though-profound concept, but there are four very important factors which, rightly understood and applied, will
contribute greatly to an understanding of this great
adventure.

BE SURE YOU ARE FILLED (CONTROLLED) BY THE SPIRIT

In order to walk in the Spirit, *we must first be sure
that we are filled with the Spirit*. In Ephesians 5:18
(KJV), we are admonished, "Be not drunk with wine,
wherein is excess; but be filled with the spirit." To be
filled with the Holy Spirit is to be controlled and empowered by the Holy Spirit moment by moment, as a way
of life. We cannot have two masters.[1] There is a
"throne," a control center, in every life—either self (ego)
or Christ is on that throne.

We need to remember two important words: God's
command—"be ye filled"—*constantly and continually
controlled and empowered*—by the Holy Spirit; and
God's *promise*—if we ask anything according to God's
will, He hears us, and if He hears us, He answers us.[2]

On the authority of God's command we know that
we are praying according to His will when we claim
His fullness by faith. Therefore, we can expect Him to
fill and empower us on the basis of His command and
promise—provided we genuinely desire to surrender
the control of our lives to Christ, and trust Him to fill
us. Technically, we are filled as an act of faith—not by
asking to be filled—in the same way that we become
Christians by faith, according to Ephesians 2:8,9 (and
not because we ask Christ to come into our lives).

Forgiveness and cleansing from sin are the results of confession. 1 John 1:9 reminds us, "But if we confess our sins to Him, He can be depended on to forgive us and to cleanse us from every wrong" (TLB). Confession means *to agree* with God concerning our sins in three ways: (1) Anything that is contrary to God's Word and will is sin; (2) Christ died and shed His blood for our sins; (3) Repentance, which means, "I change my attitude toward my sin," results in a Godward change in my actions toward that sin. Continue to breathe spiritually as a way of life, "exhaling" (confessing, then acknowledging God's love and forgiveness) whenever the Holy Spirit reveals a sin which you need to confess, and "inhaling" (appropriating, by faith, the fullness and control of the Holy Spirit) as you continue to walk in the Spirit.

WHAT ABOUT EMOTION?

Avoid being unduly introspective. Do not probe within yourself, looking for sin to confess. Confess only what the Holy Spirit impresses you to confess. Do not seek an emotional experience. If you genuinely hunger and thirst after God and His righteousness, and if you have confessed your sin, surrendered the control of your life to Christ, and claimed the fullness of the Holy Spirit by faith, you can *know* that you are filled with the Holy Spirit. Christ is now on the throne of your life. God will prove Himself faithful to His promise.

Do not depend upon feelings—the Christian is to live by faith, trusting in the trustworthiness of God Himself and His Word. This can be illustrated by a train diagram. Let us call the engine *fact*—the fact of God's promises found in His Word. The coal car we will call *faith*—our trust in God and His Word. The caboose we will call *feelings*.

It would be futile to attempt to pull the train by the caboose. In the same way we, as Christians, do not depend upon feelings or emotions. In order to live a Spirit-filled life we simply place our faith in the fact that God and His Word are trustworthy. Feelings will eventually follow in the life of faith,[3] but we should never depend on feelings or look for them. The very act of looking for an emotional experience is a denial of the concept of faith, and whatever is not of faith is sin.[4]

You can know right now that you are under the Holy Spirit's loving care by trusting God, His *command* and *promise*, and you can go through life with that joyful assurance.

SPIRITUAL CONFLICT

Second, *we must be prepared for spiritual conflict* if we expect to walk in the control of the Holy Spirit.

We are told in 1 Peter 5:7,8 to let God have all our worries and cares, for He is always thinking about us and watching everything that concerns us. We are to be careful—watching out for attacks from Satan, our great enemy, who prowls around like a hungry roaring lion looking for some victim to tear apart. Satan is a real foe and we need to be alert to his cunning and subtle ways as well as to obvious attempts to defeat and destroy us. But we can have confidence knowing that "greater is He who is in you than he who is in the world."[5] I once used this illustration to explain to a friend why he need not fear Satan. "What do you do with lions in your city?" I said. He replied, "We put them in a cage at the zoo." I said, "Visit the cage in the zoo and watch a lion pacing impatiently back and forth. He cannot hurt you if you are careful. But if you get in that cage the lion will make mincemeat of you. You have nothing to fear so long as you stay out of that cage."

Satan is in a "cage." Two thousand years ago Satan was defeated when our Lord Jesus Christ died on the cross for our sins. Victory is *now* ours. We do not look forward to victory but we move *from* victory—the victory of the cross. You have nothing to fear from Satan so long as you depend upon Christ and not on your own strength. Remember, Satan has no power over you except that which God in His wisdom and grace allows him to have.[6]

KNOW YOUR RIGHTS AS A CHILD OF GOD

Third, if we are going to walk in the Spirit, we *need to know our rights as children of God.* We need to know how to draw upon the inexhaustible resources of God's love, wisdom, power, forgiveness and abundant grace.

One of the most important things that we can do to learn about our rights as children of God is to spend much time in reading, studying, memorizing and meditating on the Word of God, and in prayer and witnessing. When Christ takes up residence in our lives, our bodies become temples of God. God's Word tells us that all authority in heaven and earth belongs to Christ[7] and we are complete in Him.[8] When we have Christ we have everything we need. Jesus promised special power to live holy lives and to be effective witnesses for Christ when we are controlled and empowered by Christ.[9]

At the same time we must remember that "the just

shall live by faith."[10] Many Christians think of *works* (Bible study, prayer and other spiritual disciplines) as the *means* to the life of faith. In truth they are the *results of such a life*.

LIFE OF FAITH

Fourth, if we are to walk in the Spirit, *we must live by faith*. It is sad to see wonderful, sincere Christians who have been deceived by a wrong emphasis on emotions. I know of nothing that has caused so much defeat and divisiveness among Christians. We do not live by feelings, but by faith. According to Hebrews 11:6, "Without faith it is impossible to please Him." In Galatians 3:11, Paul reminds us, "We live by faith."

In Romans 8:28 we find a promise of God to which most Christians give at least intellectual agreement: "All things work together for good to those who love God, to those who are called according to His purpose." Do you believe this promise of God? If so, you logically acknowledge the reasonableness of the following command of God in 1 Thessalonians 5:18: "In everything give thanks; for this is God's will for you in Christ Jesus."

Have you learned to say, "Thank you, Lord," when you heart is broken because of the loss of a loved one? Do you thank God when your body is wracked with pain? When you receive a "Dear John" letter terminating a love relationship? When you have financial reverses?

You may say that only a fool would give thanks to God under such circumstances. No, not if all things work together for good for those who love God. If God has commanded us to give thanks, there is a reason for it. And let me tell you, as one who has some experience in this area, this is one of the most exciting lessons that I have ever learned—the lesson of saying "thank you" when things go wrong, even when my heart is broken—sometimes through my tears.

Why should a Christian desire to walk in the control of the Holy Spirit moment by moment? First, it is a command of God. And second, by continually yielding control of the throne of your life to Christ, you will please and honor Him, who delights to have fellowship with His children; you will enjoy a fuller, richer, more exciting life with our Savior and with others; and you will overflow with God's joy as your life becomes a fruitful witness for Him.

1. Matthew 6:24; 2. 1 John 5:14,15; 3. John 14:21; 4. Hebrews 11:6; Romans 14:23; 5. 1 John 4:4b; 6. Acts 4:28; 7. Matthew 28:18; 8. Colossians 3:10; 9. Acts 1:8; 10. Romans 1:17, KJV.

APPENDIX D

A SAMPLE THREE-MINUTE TESTIMONY

Professional author/speaker Lee Roddy has shared his personal testimony through the pages of Worldwide Challenge *magazine. This article is a good example of a three-minute testimony, which we encourage all Christians to write.*

As a former newspaper editor, I was a skeptic. My work required that I always look for evidence. I couldn't just believe what somebody told me about something. I had to know the facts. The best way I could do that was check them out myself.

So I was skeptical one morning several years ago when a friend began talking about knowing Jesus Christ in a personal way. He and I were members of the same denomination, both extremely active, but I had never heard anybody talk like that.

He invited me to a laymen's Bible study at 6:30 Thursday mornings. As I got involved, I realized that something was missing in my spiritual life. Yet it took me a long time to believe it was really possible to have a personal relationship with Jesus Christ.

I began to probe very carefully into the lives of people who professed to have this kind of relationship. I found they were real. Their lives were changed.

I talked to a man who used to be one of the biggest "partying" men in town. After he became a Christian, he had gone home and poured all his expensive liquor down the drain.

I saw other evidences of change in his life, too, as God began to give him a spirit of gentleness and love.

The men in our Bible study loved me even though I was hard on them. I asked them penetrating questions that could have made them mad. Instead, one fellow used to put his arm around me and say, "I love you, Brother." Nobody had ever done that before.

These men loved me. They'd sit and talk with me. When I had some problems, they helped me. They were consistent like that on a day-to-day basis.

Bit by bit, I became convinced, though I never had a sweeping revelation. It's like my wife and me—I can't tell you the day I fell in love with her, but we've been married thirty-nine years, and it gets better all the time.

I think the same thing is true of my relationship with Jesus Christ. The more I understood, the more I loved Him. Finally, I made a full and total commitment to Him.

That happened one day when I was home alone. I knelt and committed myself to Christ. Then I asked, "Lord, what do you want me to do with the rest of my life?"

It wasn't dramatic, yet I had a strong impression that I was to use my spiritual gift of teaching (Ephesians 4:11,12), to write, travel and lecture.

At the time, I'd been writing for about 38 years without selling any of eleven books I'd completed. My farthest travels had been to Hawaii. I had never given a lecture. But I wrote my commitment and "call" on the flyleaf of my Bible and stepped out on faith.

Since then, my wife and family say they've seen fantastic changes in my life. I think, in all honesty, that's true. Just to talk about loving Jesus Christ is a change. I used to feel funny saying things like that.

I didn't particularly love anybody. I was very self-centered. I didn't get married for a long time because I said I didn't want a wife holding me back. Of course, that was silly, but that's the way I was.

Almost immediately after my commitment, I started writing a few things for Christian publications, radio and films. Within two years, a publisher bought one of my books. Thirteen have been bestsellers, films, television programs, book club selections or award winners, such as "Jesus" and "Grizzly Adams."

My travels have taken me to Europe, Asia, Canada and Mexico.

Within a year after my commitment, I gave my first lecture and then spoke across our country. I've just contracted to speak nationally to "Fortune 500" executives, other businessmen and schools.

God continues to open doors both in Christian and secular fields. Every offer that comes in I lay before the Lord and ask, "What do You think?" Then I work by priorities.

I don't do it for money or prestige, but because the opportunities are gifts from Him. So it's awesome to realize that I can be a scribe and a speaker-teacher for the King of Kings; I, who was once such a skeptic.

Lee Roddy
Author/Speaker
19109 Swallow Way
Penn Valley, CA 95946

APPENDIX E
RESOURCES FOR PERSONAL EVANGELISM AND DISCIPLESHIP

FOR PERSONAL EVANGELISM

Have You Heard of the Four Spiritual Laws? *Bill Bright.* One of the most effective and widely used evangelistic tools ever developed, the Four Spiritual Laws gives you a meaningful, easy-to-use way of sharing your faith with others.

Would You Like To Know God Personally? A new version of the Four Spiritual Laws, presented as four principles for establishing a personal relationship with God through Jesus Christ.

Your Life Can Become a Great Adventure (The Van Dusen Letter). *Bill Bright.* This popular evangelistic tool is based on a real letter sent to a prominent businessman. It emphasizes the key issues in making a decision for Christ and includes Scripture verses and assurance review.

Jesus and the Intellectual. *Bill Bright.* Investigates the claims of Christ and the validity of Christianity from an intellectual and felt need point of view. *Jesus and the Intellectual* includes Bible verses and a four-point outline of the gospel. It's a useful evangelistic and follow-up tool.

Good News Comic Book (Children). Introduce children to Christ with this colorful gospel story. Children can use it to share with other children. It's an excellent gift for birthdays or holidays.

How to Get Better Grades and Have More Fun (High School and College). *Steve Douglass.* Here's what every student is looking for: help from a Harvard MBA for getting better grades and spending less time doing it. It gives practical guidance to help all students raise their grade point average, deal with stress and manage their time. Includes a clear presentation of the gospel. Fast reading and easy to apply.

How to Achieve Your Potential and Enjoy Life (Adult). *Steve Douglass.* Written by a Harvard MBA in the popular style of *How to Get Better Grades and Have More Fun,* this book helps adults who want to find success and fulfillment. Practical, motivational, and with a clear presentation of the gospel. An ideal book to share with your non-Christian friends.

Tell It Often, Tell It Well. *Mark McCloskey.* You can gain confidence and practical help to initiate sharing your Christian faith with others through this motivating and insightful book. It is a well-reasoned, biblical approach to fruitful witnessing, and is used as a text in several Bible colleges and seminaries.

FOR PERSONAL DISCIPLESHIP

Transferable Concepts. *Bill Bright.* These booklets explain the "how-to's" of consistent, successful Christian living. They're great for personal follow-up and discipleship. They are also available as one conveniently bound paperback entitled *Transferable Concepts for Powerful Living.*

How To Be Sure You Are a Christian
How To Experience God's Love and
    Forgiveness
How To Be Filled With The Spirit
How To Walk In The Spirit
How To Pray

Five Steps to Christian Growth. Establishes new believers in five cornerstones of the faith: assurance of salvation, steps to growing, understanding God's love, experiencing God's forgiveness and being filled with the Spirit.

Ten Basic Steps Toward Christian Maturity. *Bill Bright.* These eleven individual booklets from the *Handbook for Christian Maturity* cover practical, biblical steps to developing your Christian walk.

Introduction—The Uniqueness of Jesus
Step 1—The Christian Adventure
Step 2—The Christian and the Abundant
    Life
Step 3—The Christian and the Holy
    Spirit
Step 4—The Christian and Prayer
Step 5—The Christian and the Bible
Step 6—The Christian and Obedience
Step 7—The Christian and Witnessing
Step 8—The Christian and Stewardship
Step 9—Highlights of the Old Testament

Step 10—Highlights of the New Testament

Transferable Concepts for Powerful Living. *Bill Bright.* This book will give you and your disciples the help you need for a consistent and victorious Christian walk. Previously available only as Transferable Concepts booklets, these lessons are now compiled into one convenient study guide. Discover the ten most important ingredients for enriching your spiritual life and learn ways to pass this vital information on to others.

Handbook for Christian Maturity. *Bill Bright.* As the follow-up material for the nationwide Power for Living campaign, this book has fostered new life and growth among individuals and study groups looking for practical help in understanding the Christian life. You'll focus on the ten most essential building blocks for developing a strong walk of faith.

The 31-Day Experiment: A Personal Experiment in Knowing God. *Dick Purnell.* A thought-provoking, yet easy-to-use prayer and Bible study guide to help you cultivate your walk with God. You'll develop the habit of a consistent daily time with the Lord.

Promises: A Daily Guide to Supernatural Living. *Bill Bright.* A daily devotional guide to help change your life. Live a supernatural life every day by meditating and acting upon God's promises.

Discipling the Young Person. *Paul Fleischmann, editor.* Practical help from fifteen of America's top youth workers. Winner of the ECPA Gold Medallion award.